The Creative Process

CAROL BURKE
JOHNS HOPKINS UNIVERSITY

MOLLY BEST TINSLEY
U.S. NAVAL ACADEMY

ST. MARTIN'S PRESS   New York

Senior editor: Catherine Pusateri
Managing editor: Patricia Mansfield-Phelan
Project editor: Talvi Laev
Production supervisor: Katherine Battiste
Art director: Sheree L. Goodman
Text design: Gene Crofts
Cover design: Hothouse Design, Inc.
Cover art: "Drawing Hands" (1948), © M. C. Escher/Cordon Art, Baarn, Holland

Library of Congress Catalog Card Number: 92-50043

Manufactured in the United States of America.

7 6 5 4 3
f e d c b a

For information, write:

St. Martin's Press, Inc.
175 Fifth Avenue
New York, NY 10010

ISBN: 0-312-06117-X

Acknowledgments

Nancy Arbuthnot: "Late Spring" by Nancy Arbuthnot. First appeared in *Shenandoah.* Reprinted with permission of the author.

Elizabeth Bishop: Excerpt from "Roosters" from *The Complete Poems, 1927–1979* by Elizabeth Bishop. Copyright © 1979, 1983 by Alice Helen Methfessel. Reprinted by permission of Farrar, Straus & Giroux, Inc.

Evan S. Connell: Excerpt from "El Dorado," from *A Long Desire.* Copyright © 1979 by Evan S. Connell Jr. Published by North Point Press and reprinted by permission of Farrar, Straus & Giroux, Inc.

Geraldine Connolly: "Godmothers" by Geraldine Connolly. Copyright © Geraldine Connolly, 1988. This poem appeared in *The Red Room* (Heatherstone Press, 1988) and *Food for the Winter* (Purdue University Press, 1990). Reprinted by permission of the author.

Acknowledgments and copyrights are continued at the back of the book on pages 177–178, which constitute an extension of the copyright page.

Preface

The Creative Process springs directly from our experience in the introductory creative writing classroom and workshop. It expresses our conviction that powerful writing flowers when we respect and nurture the nonlinear, intuitive creative process rather than analyze and prescribe formulae for finished products.

For years, we were skeptical of textbooks, thinking that they tended to sound either too confident and mechanical or too vague and inspirational. We knew creative writing didn't lend itself to an organized, checklist approach, nor did it necessarily follow an onrush of strong feelings and intentions. So, year after year, we photocopied a progressive sequence of exercises, ordered anthologies of contemporary poems, stories, and essays, and addressed general issues of content, technique, and genre as they arose in particular pieces of student writing.

This approach worked in our classes. It not only produced authentic writing, but it also offered a lively, meaningful experience to all willing participants, not just the few who already planned to pursue creative writing as a vocation.

Our approach assumes that the beginning writer's time is best spent, first, in practicing open-ended, exploratory writing, and second, in avidly sampling a wide array of work by experienced writers. Of least importance are abstract pronouncements on how to write—they mean nothing to the beginner without personal, concrete knowledge of the process to which they refer. These are the values we have tried to embody in this book.

The creative process is disorderly and recursive. It enlists mental faculties beyond the range of consciousness. It follows impulse. It defies closure on any terms but its secret own. The thirteen chapters of this book imply an order that corresponds only loosely to the actual creative experience. We urge both instructors and students to browse through its topics, seeking directions that seem most meaningful and productive. In our experience, focusing on the conventions of a particular genre is not important in the early stages of a writing course. Rather, we emphasize ways to achieve the originality and power common to all strong writing regardless of genre. Yet, if a particular reader prefers to get a feel for one genre right away, or after a week or two of less structured writing, flipping through to the appropriate chapter is very much in order.

At the same time, it is crucial to spend plenty of time experimenting, writing freely and uncritically in response to the various stimuli offered in Part One, "Discovering Material." Most beginning writers don't realize the depth and extent of their own resources: as they learn to catch their observations, memories, and daydreams on paper, they encounter unexpected people, places, things, and events. Each of us is a living treasury of fresh subjects, which Part One aims to explore.

At the core of each chapter is a series of exercises designed to give the student concrete experience with the abstract principle or process being explained. We encourage students to write fully in response to at least one as they read and to return to the others in future assignments; these will furnish the material for group discussion in regular workshops. At the end of each chapter, there are abundant shorter exercises called Notebook Options. These are aimed at stimulating daily entries in a writer's notebook in order to build the student's repertory and reserves.

In place of drama, the traditional third genre in most texts on creative writing, we have included the essay. We find it to be much more amenable to the novice writer's command than the play, given the extra layer of technical issues that theatrical production adds. We also believe the creativity of the contemporary essay to be unappreciated, particularly by students in college writing courses. Their essays are squeezed into boxes and labeled by rhetorical model (process analysis, cause and effect), then prodded for thesis statements and topic sentences, then perhaps even outlined, before everyone gives them up for dead. Thus each of our chapters introduces examples from essays as well as from poems and stories to illustrate the sources and techniques of creative writing. The final chapter presents the essay as a legitimate sibling of the poem and the story, just as rich in possibilities, the appealing product of open-ended exploration and creative technique.

We wish to thank the teachers and writers who encouraged this text and offered comments on it in their reviews: Barbara Bloom, Cabrillo College; Richard Chess, University of South Carolina; Judith Cohen, Lesley College; Gregory Garret, Baylor University; Burton Hatlen, University of Maine; Lynn Kostoff, Frances Marion College; Richard Maxwell, Foothill College; James McMichael, University of California–Irvine; Don Morril, University of Tampa; Jane Lunin Peril, Providence College; Eileen Pollack, Tufts University; Wayne Ude, Old Dominion University; and Luke Whisnant, East Carolina University. Our colleagues Harriet Bergmann and Nancy Arbuthnot generously granted us their time and helpful ideas. We are also indebted to editors Mark Gallaher and

The Creative Process

Laynie Browne for their astute guidance at various stages of the writing process, and to Talvi Laev for overseeing the production of this book.

Finally, we are most grateful to our students, who were the first to try these exercises and who learned to trust the creative process.

Carol Burke
Molly Best Tinsley

Contents

The Creative Process

PART ONE

Discovering Material

Chapter 1

Envisioning the Process

I write because it is the only way I am willing to survive.
William Saroyan, "Why I Write"

I write entirely to find out what I'm thinking, what I'm looking at, what I see and what it means.
Joan Didion, "Why I Write"

Creative writers write because they can't not write. They are moved by a pressure that has nothing to do with course credits or deadlines and much to do with exploration and discovery, with the allure of such questions as Who am I? and What is this world I inhabit about? *Creative writing* pursues all the delightful, astonishing, disturbing answers to these questions.

Creative writers celebrate the subjective, the fact that each of us has a different understanding of truth, a different vision of reality. They aim in their writing to express the vision that is distinctively theirs; they infuse it with the energy and authority of their own concrete experiences, the observations only they can offer. They know that power and originality begin with the specifically, even humbly, personal.

Notice what we have not said: Creative writers are the gifted few who plan to dedicate their future to producing literary art. Every one of us responds to life by developing a special *vision,* a way of looking at ourselves and the people and objects around us that determines what we see. We all move through "a world of our own" though most of the time we tend to assume ours is the same as everyone else's, downplaying its peculiarities in order to keep communal business running smoothly. Creative writing is first of all a matter of becoming conscious of this private world, believing in its uniqueness and significance, exploring it to its farthest reaches, then articulating sharply and honestly what we find. Whereas we

3

have spent our lives within its boundaries, and may find it a little predictable or boring, to someone else it represents new territory, secret and strange.

When we say that creative writing is self-centered, we are pointing out its source of life; we are not prescribing subject matter. In fact, creative writing embraces the most diverse and apparently "selfless" array of topics—great-aunts, old running shoes, Lyndon Baines Johnson or Magic Johnson, an apple orchard. Nor are we recommending self-indulgence. Some students may pick up this book secretly hoping that if they are creative enough in their thoughts and intentions, they will manage somehow to avoid the writing part, which is still, after all, hard work. Others may be in the habit of writing only in a state of inspiration, and may feel somewhat put off by our enthusiasm for sheer quantity in writing, for regularly jotting down everything they perceive, remember, and dream. Our first principle is simple: We learn about writing by writing. Increments in quantity lead to increments in quality. As the Romantic poet William Blake declared, "The Road of Excess leads to the Palace of Wisdom."

If our first commandment is *Write,* our second is *Don't forget your audience.* No matter how attractive we may find the image of the alienated artist, contemptuous of the misunderstanding masses, we write for others as well as for ourselves. Deny it as we might, we write because we want to go public. We do want people to say, "I know just what you mean; you've expressed perfectly something I've been vaguely thinking about." Or "I know that woman in your story; she's just like my grandmother."

For the creative writer, the exhilaration of self-expression and the desire to communicate often pull against each other. The resulting tension is productive and makes all the more valuable the sharing of writing, especially with other serious writers in a group workshop. Response to our writing can help us identify strengths and pinpoint weaknesses; as we read aloud, we can hear pleasure, amusement, surprise, and disgust in the small sounds our audience makes, or we may look up and catch someone covering a yawn.

Offering work to the scrutiny of a group can feel frightening and confusing unless the members of the workshop agree on certain ground rules. Participants must understand, first of all, how much listeners' initial responses may be influenced by personal taste, how often they may disagree on the effect or value of a passage, and how pointless it becomes to wrangle over these differences. Better simply to allow divergent opinions to coexist, and leave final resolutions to the writer. Members must also remember to focus responses on the writing, rather than on the writer or on a real-world issue that may have found its way into the writing. The author of a story about an alcoholic will not be helped by hearing a discourse on willpower or twelve-step programs.

Perhaps most important, the members of a workshop must agree that its purpose is mutual encouragement. This does not mean listeners should praise everything, but it does mean that they should acknowledge the good points in a piece of writing. It also means that classmates should present comments as subjective description, rather than objective judgment: for example, they might explain that a particular image is too familiar or that the ending of a particular story does not meet their expectations, rather than pronounce the image a cliché or the ending a flop.

Essentially, the listener in a workshop charts his or her responses and feeds back to the reader a picture of the peaks and troughs and flats. The listener points out the parts that amused, surprised, or disappointed; the parts that provoked curiosity, excitement, impatience; the parts that were confusing; and the parts that were clear.

It takes commitment and weeks of practice to get this process working productively, but finally, alert listeners become more alert writers. As members gain experience being the audience, the importance of audience to a writer becomes more real and clear. Besides the exchange of information, the act of reading aloud, of relinquishing a piece of the private world to the public, has its own special effect. It is a way of cutting certain ties between writer and work, intimate ties like those that prevent a parent from being objective about his or her child. After presenting writing in a workshop, a writer is able to see it more clearly and make the judgments that revision will require.

Our third and last commandment is *Read*. Nothing will challenge and expand a writer's talents more than exposure to the particular innovations of professional writers. This book is best conceived as a supplement, a travelogue to accompany a continuous creative expedition into literary quarterlies and anthologies, where you will find plenty of living examples of the principles and techniques described in these chapters. (*Best American Short Stories* and *Best American Essays* are published in paperback every year by Houghton Mifflin; Macmillan publishes the annual *Best American Poetry* collection. The yearly *Pushcart Prize Anthology*, published by Viking, offers outstanding stories, poems, and essays gathered from literary magazines around the country.) In these samples, you will see things you will want to try yourself and things you think you can do better; you will remember things you forgot you knew. Sharing the visions of others, you will expand and clarify your own.

Creative Looping

*Implicit in the concept of Strange Loops is the concept of infinity,
since what else is a loop but a way of representing an endless
process in a finite way?*

Douglas R. Hofstadter, *Gödel, Escher, Bach*

*A writer is not so much someone who has something to say as he
is someone who has found a process that will bring about new
things he would not have thought of if he had not started to say
them.*

William Stafford, "Writing"

Teachers and psychologists who have studied the writing process
have suggested that it occurs in two stages. The key to the first is
freedom—freedom from judgment and censure, from the rules of "correct"
writing; freedom to write down any and all images and ideas that a given
subject stimulates, to whip up a brainstorm and fly into its eye. Once the
assorted images and ideas have been put into words on paper, the second
stage can begin. Spontaneity gives way to logical analysis; the writer
appraises the material generated in stage one and establishes the objec-
tives which will guide him or her in focusing, shaping, polishing, and
correcting it. The first stage might be likened to a sculptor preparing a
quantity of molding clay or a wood carver choosing and stripping a log.
Once an artist has gathered an amorphous bulk of material, he or she can
move on to the process of discovering and bringing out its potential.

This model is helpful in the way it identifies the different, even
conflicting, tasks a writer must perform. Separating these tasks into stages
honors the importance of spontaneous creativity in the writing process
and highlights the importance of revision. In other words, it isn't the
rhyme scheme that produces a good sonnet; nor is it the comparison-
contrast format that produces a lively essay. The perfect stanza or paragraph does not leap fully formed from the writer's brain; rather it is the
result of much experimentation—tightening and expansion, rewording
and reordering, through draft after draft.

Unfortunately, the two-stage model for writing doesn't take us much
further into the mysteries of the creative process than that. In fact, the
following chapters in this book have been arranged to suggest three stages:
the first four focus on *generating material;* the middle four, on exploring
that material for possibilities, experimenting, and *discovering a general
direction;* and the last four, on *shaping and structuring,* once certain preliminary decisions have been made. However, this sequence only loosely
approximates the order in which we approach a creative writing project.

Some writers push themselves to write through to the end of a work simply in order to see what its general size, shape, and direction are going to be. They refer to this roughest of drafts as a *zero-draft* to emphasize its tentativeness. But there are times when it doesn't feel right to force a complete zero-draft before going back to begin shaping and revising. The truth is, as creative writers, we are always doing a little of everything all at once.

In a lithograph entitled *Drawing Hands,* the artist M. C. Escher portrays just that—a right hand penciling in the shirtcuff from which emerges a left hand, which is similarly penciling in the shirtcuff above the right. This visual paradox is an apt metaphor for the creative process: it defies linear logical analysis. If each hand has created the other, neither one existed before the other; then how did the process that has now advanced to the shirtcuffs ever get started? The writer might put it this way: I don't know what I've got to say until it's down on paper, but I can't start getting it down on paper until I know what I'm going to say.

It is impossible to impose a single, infallible order on creative writing. More often than not, we explore material as we generate it; we begin to shape and direct it before we know what we've got. At the same time that we are sinking into an image, scene, or example, developing its details, we are looking ahead, guessing ahead as to which details might reinforce a meaning, of which we are as yet only vaguely aware. We are in uncharted territory, and we have to do a lot of guessing and trusting intuitions.

If the self is the pumping heart of creative writing, then intuition is its blood, and this book is a course in aerobics. It is full of exercises, but they are not rigid assignments. They do not imply rights and wrongs. Though their element of arbitrary structure may seem "counterintuitive," it actually serves to lull the conscious mind and release the less-conscious intuitive processes—much the way bright ideas seem always to flash forth when we are driving along a familiar highway.

The Question of Genre

Although many of the exercises in this book return you to the facts, persons, places, and instances of your "real life," you are encouraged to combine and manipulate this *raw* material as well as to invent new material when your writer's intuition urges it. These exercises are first-stage stimuli designed to help you discover and develop your own personal vision. Issues of factual or scientific accuracy can be postponed until later stages of revision. In fact, in a story or poem, the sooner you let go of real life, the sooner you are free to imagine, and the more prepared you will be later to enhance the integrity and intensity of the final work. Aesthetic flaws can never be justified by the excuse "But that's what really happened."

What about the essay? Everyone knows that a poem can be pure nonsense, whereas an essay must stick to the truth, right? This rule of thumb sounds simple enough. What then do we make of these lines from William Matthews's poem "Nurse Sharks," particularly when compared to the paragraph that follows them, from Jonathan Swift's eighteenth-century essay "A Modest Proposal"?

> Since most sharks have no flotation bladders and must swim
> to keep from sinking, they like to sleep in underwater caves,
> wedged between reef-ledges, or in water so shallow
> that their dorsal fins cut up from the surf.

> I have been assured by a very knowing American of my acquaintance in London, that a young healthy child well nursed is at a year old a most delicious, nourishing, and wholesome food, whether stewed, roasted, baked, or boiled; and I make no doubt that it will equally serve in a fricassee or a ragout.

In its search for new sources of energy, creative writing repeatedly leaps genre lines, presenting us with prose poems, lyrical or encyclopedic experiments in fiction, imaginative personal essays, and narrative poems with characters and dialogue. In Thomas Pynchon's novel V, Esther undergoes a nose job, and the surgery is recounted in accurate clinical detail. In his short story "Morrison's Reaction," Stephen Kirk gives an account of escalating violence by describing in full technical terms the ordeals of Vincent at the hands of his dentist.

While complete technical accuracy is at home in fiction, many an essay has sprung from imaginative fantasy. In " 'But a Watch in the Night': A Scientific Fable," the conservationist James C. Rettie envisions a highly evolved, 757-million-year-old race of Copernicans who have used their time-lapse cameras and superpowered telescopes to make a film record of the history of life on Earth and plan to bring it to our planet "in the near future." He then previews the film, which will take exactly a year to run, in order to emphasize the devastation of the North American environment that has occurred since the United States became a nation: we Americans destroy in seven seconds what has taken a whole year to evolve.

Because the elements of powerful, original writing are universal to all genres, this book tends to de-emphasize genre distinctions until its final chapters. For many writers, it is true, choice of genre happens before anything else, almost preconsciously. It is another intuition, worth respecting, but not if it means equating the whole writing effort with the formal rules and conventions of that genre. (In fact, the last chapters in this book could be viewed as an invitation to experiment outside your "first-choice" genre, as much as instruction in how to write within it.)

Similarly, the exercises in these pages could be used to launch a novel or a play, the two genres whose special challenges lie beyond the scope of this introductory book. While the traditional novel demands of its author a competence with sustained structure or plot, as well as vast stretches of uninterrupted writing time, current literary developments have welcomed departures from that norm in the form of the novella and the linked story sequence, often billed as "a novel in stories." And no matter what the length or how elaborate the structure, the successful novel must bring characters to life and record their conflicts from an interesting, fertile point of view in a setting rich with sensory detail. Similarly, writing for the stage requires a knowledge of practical theater and its history that cannot be condensed into a single chapter on genre. Yet the vital, resonant dialogue at the heart of good theater springs from characters caught in intriguing conflict with one another and with their environment. In other words, a plot formula or a theatrical trick is no substitute for the preliminary open-ended process of free imagining and experimentation explored in these chapters.

Perhaps at this point we can venture a definition of the problematic term we have been using so freely—*creative writing*. Creative writing is open-ended writing, and thus different from technical writing or analysis written to the specifications of a particular discipline. In creative writing, we aren't sure of the objective when we begin, and we are surprised by the words and images and insights we discover or recall along the way. Finally, we judge our work not by matching it to a preexisting set of standards or a preexisting body of information but by testing its emotional impact, internal coherence, and intuitive truth.

The Writer's Notebook

A serious visual artist might carry around a sketchbook in order to catch and save the contours, gestures, and patterns the real world offers from moment to moment, day by day. Then in the isolation of the studio, when it is time to create a mini-world by putting charcoal to paper or brush to canvas, the artist has a reservoir of interesting possibilities for the foreground, as well as plenty of good stuff with which to fill in the background.

A writer's notebook has a similar purpose. There is nothing more likely to send all your thoughts and words into oblivion than the empty privacy of your own room, a blank sheet of paper, and the demand that, by tomorrow, second period, you write something brilliant or at least clever. If, however, you already have words, images, and ideas on paper, the task becomes much simpler, even enjoyable. You are no longer creating something out of nothing; your starting point is there for the choosing—perhaps several starting points that you will feel challenged to combine. You have a firm basis from which to begin your free association, your fantasies, your argument. Life has become much easier, and all because you took a moment to jot down things you saw, heard, smelled, touched, tasted, remembered, or dreamed.

The notebook is not, by the way, a daily journal. Think of yourself as a scavenger, moving through your outer and inner worlds with senses alert, particularly your sense of possibility. Think of your notebook as the receptacle for the assorted treasures you find. You might inscribe this reminder on the inside front cover: *The strongest impression is weaker than the palest ink.*

At the end of each chapter, we suggest appropriate exercises you can try in your notebook, called Notebook Options. On the one hand, they will give you practice with the approaches or techniques explained in the chapter. At the same time, they will suggest the sorts of collectibles you can look for and try for on your own.

Here are some sample entries from one writer's notebook, to give you a more specific notion of the possibilities:

> The only time you can find a screwdriver in my house is when you're looking for a hammer.

> H: It was a wonderful relationship until tonight.
> S: He's mad because he dropped garbage all over my floor, and I yelled at him.
> H: That's the last time I cook in your kitchen.
> S: You never have. (to me) He never has. It's an empty threat.
> H: I won't even boil water from now on.
> S: He's never set foot in my kitchen before tonight.

> The man lying on the sidewalk, wearing red T-shirt, red track shorts, and wornout blue tennis shoes. A flat bottle of Hennessy whiskey beside his open palm. He somehow managed, falling, not to let it drop and break. No one will touch him. We circle him trying to determine whether he's breathing. The leafy shadows of a curbside tree move across his chest, and I cannot separate their motion from what I hope is a faint lift and fall of his red shirt. No one can touch him. We are afraid. Someone warns that he might be faking. His legs are stubbly with hair like an old man's, the socks relaxed in loose

folds around his ankles. I cannot touch him. If mouth to mouth resuscitation could save his life, I doubt that I could perform it.

In the train, the cries of kids and the smell of peanut butter.

Wendell, for whom you always have to make allowances. He never does anything exactly right. It's his way of testing your affection for him. If you truly care for him, you are willing to pretend everything he does is just fine.

Like my grandmother's apartment: the smell of wet wool.

NOTEBOOK OPTIONS

1. Try to observe one of the following everyday actions and describe it in as much sensory detail as you can, preferably as it is going on: a person peeling, unwrapping, mixing, microwaving, or otherwise preparing some food, then eating it; a person pumping gas, from drive-in to drive-off; a person dressing for an athletic practice or event, or a date; ten to fifteen nonsleeping minutes in the life of a dog or cat.
2. Take a day to notice things about eyes, a day to focus on noses or mouths, and then a day to concentrate on some other part of a human being. Each day, write down your observations.
3. Begin keeping a list of the gestures people perform in conversation—what they do with their faces and bodies while they are speaking, listening, and thinking about what to say next (chewing the inside of a cheek, tearing a piece of paper into small bits, poking an ear with the tip of a car key).

Chapter 2

Working with Words

The writer must be able to feel words intimately, one at a time.
He must also be able to step back, inside his head, and see the
flowing sentence. But he starts with the single word.

Donald Hall, *Writing Well*

As toddlers we learned the life and power of language when we
realized that individual words could replace the inarticulate cry and so
identify wants and define discomforts with new precision. In conversa-
tions with other children and in the monologues that accompanied solitary play, we wielded language with increasing sophistication to (at least
imaginatively) resolve domestic conflicts, conquer evil forces, and create
worlds over which we presided. Living in a world in which words are
referential, imaginative, and therapeutic, we devised our first verbal fic-
tions in play.

But as we progressed in school, we saw the periods of play lessen and
our speech inside the classroom frequently dwindle to programmed replies
to teachers' questions. For speaking out of turn or for chatting (what a
fifth-grade teacher used to call "visiting with your neighbor"), one might
even have received punishment—missing recess to write fifty times, "I
will not talk in class."

Outside of class, on the other hand, we continued to sense that words
had the power both to influence peers and to create imagined worlds. But
we inevitably learned to distinguish the language of play from the language
of an environment dominated by adults. We learned the rules governing
the use of language often by violating them or witnessing their violation
(what anthropologists call "breaching behavior"). Even though on the
playground we might have comfortably referred to someone as a "retard," a
parent overhearing such a word might well have censured us. But even the

few who daringly or foolishly broke the rules of classroom speech learned sooner or later to tailor their words to teachers' expectations.

In writing, too, we learned to respond with "the right answer." The teacher or the textbook presented certain truths, and all too often our writing dutifully repeated those truths. On a third-grade geography test, we typically wrote a sentence or two naming the continents of the world and their contiguous oceans; we never described the exotic scene we imagined taking place on one of these large land masses. In such academic writing exercises we learned to substitute the general for the specific and to forfeit the unusual in favor of the conventional.

We all recall, of course, moments when the teacher invited us to do "creative writing," moments generally designed to produce the predictable and the clichéd, rather than the individual and the fresh. The seasonal poems ("Things I'm Thankful For" on Thanksgiving, the valentine verse, and the "abundance of spring" poems) elicited little more than imitations of greeting cards and frequently expressed the narrowest range of approved emotions and insights. Even the child wrestling with the trauma of a divorce was expected to write an affirmative, chipper poem about spring!

As a society, we regard the most famous scientists and mathematicians as highly creative individuals, yet few of us ever wrote speculatively in our science and math classes. "Creative writing" was left for the isolated English course with that title or for the single unit in an English course, with often a high premium placed on strictly patterned verse like haiku and cinquain or on the short, short story (five to seven handwritten pages), all too often with the long, long list of characters and the overly intricate plot.

Most of us have practiced *academic* writing since fourth grade and might even have gained some proficiency as academic writers, but that training has not always served to develop skills in creative writing. In some cases it may even have dulled it. Looking closely at our language, we sometimes find it hardened into the grunts of vagueness and cliché. We so easily reduce all we're feeling, thinking, and perceiving to generic phrases that cover a vast list of possibilities. We say we have a lot of *stuff* to do. We're overworked, we claim, but *things seem* to be getting better.

As writers, we must return to the mystery and the miracle of language we experienced as children, to a time when we, like our primordial parents, Adam and Eve, freshly translated the world of things into a world of words. In the following passage from the memoir "Moon on a Silver Spoon," Eudora Welty describes that Edenic moment:

> In my sensory education I include my physical awareness of the
> word. Of a certain word, this is; the connection it has with what it

stands for. Around age six, perhaps, I was standing by myself in our front yard waiting for supper, just at that hour in a late summer day when the sun is already below the horizon and the risen full moon in the visible sky stops being chalky and begins to take on light. There comes the moment, and I saw it then, when the moon goes from flat to round. For the first time it met my eyes as a globe. The word "moon" came into my mouth as though fed to me out of a silver spoon. Held in my mouth the moon became a word. It had the roundness of a Concord grape that Grandpa took off his vine and gave me to suck out of its skin and swallow whole, in Ohio.

In Welty's moment of naming, the child does not separate and distinguish words from things but connects the roundness of moon, grape, eyes, even the word *Ohio* into the startling image of consumption—and transfixes us.

As writers, we must constantly return to the basics of our craft, to individual words. Mere black marks on a page, colorless and insubstantial, individual words can create the illusion of life, of color and substance. Handled cleverly and respectfully, they do more than refer to things; they *become* those things, filling up an imagined world.

The Thingness of Words

The poet Robert Francis offers a wonderfully pure example of the "thingness" of words. Fascinated with what he calls "the strong character of solid compounds," Francis began by making lists of such words and soon found himself piecing them together into a patchwork that became "Silent Poem." As with most poems, you must read this poem aloud to fully appreciate it.

Silent Poem

backroad   leafmold   stonewall   chipmunk
underbrush   grapevine   woodchuck   shadblow

woodsmoke   cowbarn   honeysuckle   woodpile
sawhorse   bucksaw   outhouse   wellsweep

backdoor   flagstone   bulkhead   buttermilk
candlestick   ragrug   firedog   brownbread

hilltop   outcrop   cowbell   buttercup
whetstone   thunderstorm   pitchfork   steeplebush

gristmill   millstone   cornmeal   waterwheel
watercress   buckwheat   firefly   jewelweed

gravestone   groundpine   windbreak   bedrock
weathercock   snowfall   starlight   cockcrow

The effort that begins with the poet's playfulness culminates in a poem that Francis describes as "a picture of old-time New England, a picture moving from wildwood to dwelling, outdoors and in, then out and up to pasture and down to millstream." By presenting a list of single words in all their starkness with no "talk" surrounding them, Francis brings to life both the words themselves and the silence that falls between them.

Consider, for a moment, your appreciation of words. Are there words that never fail to impress you? words that sound harsh or grating? words that identify their speaker's class, regional origin, and prejudices? Can certain words be spoken in anything but anger? Are others shyly seductive? Are some fastidious and others easygoing?

In a poll of students enrolled in a writing class, one described *cellardoor* as the most beautiful word in the English language, one favored *mayonnaise*, another relished *marjoram* and *Tonawanda*. A young woman from Wyoming pronounced *luminous* slowly and mysteriously as if savoring each syllable. When asked to identify the most beautiful word in the English language, most people tend to select one with a pleasing sound (often containing "m" and "s" sounds) or one that faintly delivers a whiff of the exotic. What word would you identify as your favorite word?

Each word is ultimately unique, and the writer strives to discover the right word, *le mot juste,* that "fits" because of its hovering connotations, its sound and rhythm, and its context. Isn't there a difference between a Robert and a Bobby; a Katherine and a Kate; a Jerome and a Jerry; an Elizabeth, a Betty, a Beth, an Eliza, and a Betsy? Names invoke connotations of familiarity and respect. You would think no more of referring to your friend Jim as "Mr. Bishop" than you would have of addressing your high-school principal Ms. Garcia as "Anita."

Although *catlike* is synonymous with *feline,* and *friendly fire* means the same as *our own troops dropping bombs on us,* these words are *not* the same. When we substitute one for the other, we alter the sense of a piece of writing. Think of all the words we have at our beck and call merely to describe our use of words: *talk, retort, pontificate, boast, discuss, blab, confer, twaddle, confess, profess, gossip, chatter, shoot the breeze,* to name a few. Shuffle them around, say enough of them aloud, and soon you've got a rhythm. Or string them together with others and *soliloquize* on syllogisms, *lisp* a lecture, *blather* on about Band-Aids, *bandy* big words, or just chew the rag!

EXERCISE: Synonyms

Select a short piece of prose (at least ten sentences) from a text-book, an advertisement, a magazine or newspaper article, or a letter you've written or received. For at least one word in each sentence, substitute a synonym. What changes in your reading of the passage as a result of your substitutions?

As you write, play with individual words, substituting five or six until an image clicks, until a sentence or a line of poetry resonates like a chord. Let that resonance then echo through your composition. When you write, according to Annie Dillard, you "lay out a line of words. The line of words is a miner's pick, a woodcarver's gouge, a surgeon's probe. You wield it, and it digs a path you follow."

•   •   •

Neither the characters in your stories nor the sentiments in your poems will come to life until your words do.

> . . . You can say anything you want, yessir, but it's the words that sing, they soar and descend. . . . I bow to them. . . . I love them, I cling to them, I run them down, I bite into them, I melt them down. . . . I love words so much. . . . The unexpected ones. . . . The ones I wait for greedily or stalk until, suddenly, they drop. . . . Vowels I love. . . . They glitter like colored stones, they leap like silver fish, they are foam, thread, metal, dew. . . . I run after certain words. . . . I catch them in midflight, as they buzz past, I trap them, clean them, peel them, I set myself in front of a dish. . . .
>
> Pablo Neruda, *Memoirs*

The writer loves words—marvels at their sheer abundance and de-lights in the single word that in a well-written passage radiates across the page. Sometimes the writer collects and hoards words in the pages of note-books, saving them for just the right passage that will show them to advan-tage; at other times he or she lavishly spills them forth, free for the taking.

EXERCISE: Making Lists

Using a thesaurus, your friends' suggestions, or your own memory, list at least twenty words that fit into a single category. Choose any category you wish: the names of birds, boats, or colors; synonyms for talking, working, eating; words you associate with affection, dislike, rever-ence; whatever.

Read your list aloud, and group some of your words into an interesting rhythm. For example, a list of fish might be arranged to generate a
certain sound:

cod, haddock, mackerel, mullet, perch,
blue, blackfish, redfish, whitefish, bass,
squid, sculpin, sturgeon, sucker, sole

Returning to your own list of words, choose either to write two or
three sentences that include several items from your list or to build a poem
or piece of prose around your list. The following poem, for example,
began as a simple list of colors:

Commission

for Marcelle Toor

I spend days now
writing lines as bleached
as this Indiana landscape
with its miles of stalk stubble
mute in winter fields,
the gray corncribs along the interstate,
bellied up with feed. But, flush with the sky,
this land is too open for images
too wide for a frame.

Here, 900 miles away,
I need your colors breathing
in their borders.
Stretch me the universe
taut and echoless;
then make it swell with acrylic.
No still life can I live with;
paint me nothing I can name.

Late in this December night
I write, wishing you could
somehow flay the dark,   ,
layer after layer,
to a morning that
bleeds in its opening
and a day veined with pigment,
pied flaxen and damson;

or that you'd spill
your whole vat of blues—
I want them all: cerulean,
ultramarine, electric, steel, teal,
navy, baby, even robin's egg too—
or that you'd blazon a canvas,
that you'd coat me for the winter.

Carol Burke

• • •

The simple names of colors, of objects and their parts, even of places (like French Lick, Thorntown, and Ovid), can yield rich sources of multiple meanings to exploit. Be keenly aware of the words around you: the language of advertising, the terms that pass back and forth at the poker table, the banter in the workplace, the words in a physics text, the language of the computer.

Always be on the lookout for words you can use. Sometimes you will find these words in unusual places. Bored once at a conference in the Midwest, a friend of the authors skipped the afternoon's meetings and toured the local historical museum. Wandering through the somber galleries, dim as funeral parlors, he happened on a room of old farm tools. The objects themselves, snug in their displays, were as tedious as the conference meetings he had attended that morning. Disuse had transferred them from the farmer's comfortable grip to the silence of the display case. Although the tools seemed frozen as skeletons, their names (carefully printed on beige paper) breathed a vibrancy with words like *horn snipper, hoof trimmer,* and *flailer.* As he stood looking inside the warm lighted cases, his mind raking images through the toothed prongs of the tools, he delighted in their anthropomorphic parts, their *cheeks, claws, faces, adz eyes,* and *necks.* He learned, for example, that the distance between a saw's toe and heel is filled with teeth, and that a rabbit plane has two seats for its plane iron—one seat for ordinary cutting, the other for close corners.

Indulge in the words around you; submit to them, even the technical words and names of everyday objects—from haircurlers to hubcaps. But shy away from the misty, sentimental "poetic" words that come easily to mind and the erudite words novices often use to sound "writerly." By trying to write about roses, one takes on the great burden of Western literary tradition. Sunsets and shimmering streams, like roses, also plod along with the heavy thud of cliché. The writer, striving to revitalize words, will find it much easier to say something fresh and interesting about hubcaps than about roses.

EXERCISE: **Appropriating Words**

Select something you routinely buy (for example, deodorant, tennis shoes, cough medicine), something you think you might buy (a new car, a pregnancy text, camping gear), or something you only fantasize buying (a hot motorcycle, a vacation in Asia, a designer dress or suit). Looking at brochures, magazine and newspaper ads, and television spots, collect as many words and phrases describing this object as you can (at least ten).

Use words from your list to write a paragraph or poem extolling the virtues of this product.

• • •

Notice how technical words work in the following poem to convince us of the speaker's fascination with the object he describes. The speaker here delights in the accumulation of detail like the consumer relishing the special features of an anticipated purchase:

Needs

I want something suited to my special needs
I want chrome hubcaps, pin-on attachments
and year round use year after year
I want a workhorse with smooth uniform cut,
dozer blade and snow blade & deluxe steering
wheel
I want something to mow, throw snow, tow, and sow with
I want precision reel blades
I want a console-styled dashboard
I want an easy spintype recoil starter
I want combination bevel and spur gears, 14
gauge stamped steel housing and
washable foam element air cleaner
I want a pivoting front axle and extrawide turf tires
I want an inch of foam rubber inside a vinyl
covering
and especially if it's not too much, if I
can deserve it, even if I can't pay for it
I want to mow while riding

A. R. Ammons

A Note on Parts of Speech

Words vary in their potential energy. One way to picture their different capacities is to rank them according to *parts of speech*. In general, verbs are stronger than nouns, which are stronger than adjectives, followed by adverbs, and, finally, prepositions. Verbs reign supreme: unlike any other part of speech, a verb can make a sentence all by itself, and a commanding one at that. Collect lists of interesting verbs, but avoid forms of the verb *be* and other plain verbs. The easiest way to transform dull, limp writing into forceful expression is to replace forms of the verb *be*, passive verbs, and flaccid verbs like *show, seem, indicate*, and so on, into strong active verbs. For example:

> Out there where the corn blades *are* more golden than any fall leaves . . .
>
> Out there where the corn blades *burn* more golden than any fall leaves . . .

Whenever possible, *think* in terms of verbs. Load your meaning into them. Beware of the bland verb paired with a five-dollar noun: *make a nomination* rather than *nominate* and *practice cooperation* rather than *cooperate*. Resist the urge to demote verbs into adjectives by casting them as participles: *the crashing waves* rather than *the waves crash* and *the humming engine* rather than *the engine hums*. Beware of any tendency to clarify dull verbs by means of adverbs (*went quietly* rather than *sneaked*) and to intensify writing with dull adverbs like *very* and *extremely*. Check over a draft to see if you rely on prepositions to clarify blah verbs: *put in, put out, put over, put on, put through*, for example.

Regard these suggestions as rules of thumb to be suspended whenever issues of style or voice dictate. By all means, don't obsess about them when getting lines or paragraphs down for the first time, though a little verb-worship, in the form of making lists of verbs and paying attention to those you encounter day to day, may intensify the way those first jottings lay themselves out on paper.

NOTEBOOK OPTIONS

1. Use your notebooks to collect as many lists of related words as you can. Note the versatility of common words. Choose a common word like *play, fall, spring, take*, or *flag*, and look it up in a dictionary or thesaurus to appreciate the way in which meanings of a word can pull against one another. *To play*, for example, suggests spontaneity; *a play* in football is

absolutely planned. This tension within words themselves underlies the pun.

Invent a paragraph using five or six different meanings of the same common word.

2. The following ad appeared in the classified section of the *Ithaca Journal* in the early 1970s:

FOR SALE: Model No. 99 Phlugerhagen with removable flam. Has four uploos that reverse to make contact with the lerk. Standard sitzen and cloggen that revolve counter clockwise. Riggletoggle and clutchritter included if desired. Battery operated piddlebottom is bit worn and gets wet, but powder will correct, Krantzer and Flipingert just overhauled. Low on cash and must part with this wonderful thing. Make offer. Address: Box 765, Care *The Ithaca Journal*

Either write a letter to the owner in which you inquire further about this marvelous item and offer to buy or swap, or write your own ad filled with equally ridiculous fake technical language.

3. Make lists of words you associate with your mother, your father, a prized possession, or a close friend. Using that list, write a paragraph or a short poem.

4. List twenty-five of your favorite adjectives. Beside each, note one or two strong verbs that come to mind, for example:

barren: scorch, wither
arrogant: boast, strut
fragile: snap, fracture

Write one short paragraph using as many of the adjectives as you can and another one with the verbs. How are the paragraphs different?

5. Ask ten friends to select what they feel is the most beautiful word in the English language, and jot down their selections. Alternatively, try the same with their least favorites. Include as many of these words as you can into a poem or paragraph about words.

6. Allow yourself the license to free-associate, stringing together long lists of words that fit together according to some "intuitive" logic, for example:

saying mass, en masse, mass hysteria, mass construction, mass transit, massive, Massachusetts, masticate, masturbate, master, mistress, mastery, mystery, missed her, hurry, Mister Muster

Chapter 3

Coming to Our Senses

Why do I write about him? Because he is and is not I. Because in the look he gives me I see myself in a way that can be written. Otherwise what would this writing be but a kind of moaning, now high, now low? When I write about him I write about myself. When I write about his dog I write about myself; when I write about the house I write about myself. Man, house, dog: no matter what the work, through it I stretch out a hand to you.

J. M. Coetzee, *Age of Iron*

Creative writing begins with dedicated *sensory perception,* a reverence for the inexhaustible stream of data about the physical world and other people that flows like an undercurrent through our conscious lives. Yet sensory perception is so primal and automatic, so available, that the beginning writer may dismiss it as a source of material. How could the clutter on my desk, one writer might ask—the rumpled papers, dull pencils, dry pens, unheeded stick 'em notes, stacked or splayed books, a plum and a wrapped muffin for lunch—how could any of this relate to the profound feeling or idea I am struggling to express? Caught up in the global affairs of the front page, the beginning writer may pass over the revealing, ongoing drama of the local news.

This chapter returns us to our senses, encourages us to indulge them, stretch and test them, and of course, record what we find. Finally, it asks us to think and feel and speak through them, to trust the sensory image even more than we do the word.

No matter how intense the emotion, no matter how firm the opinion that drives us to write, when we focus exclusively or even directly on analyzing that emotion or asserting that opinion, we produce vague abstraction. When we rely on words like *passion, despair, confusion, bliss,* when we make judgments like *unfair, stupid, irrational, excellent,* we are actually naming abstract ideas. We are presenting conclusions about experiences, leaving our readers to guess about specific circumstances and grope for associations to their own memories. In the absence of rich sensory data, our readers will never have to leave the safe, familiar world of their own assumptions and stereotypes; they will have their automatic or "knee-jerk" responses to our subject and then dismiss it. What an abstract pronouncement does is skip over the complex experience itself, offering readers nothing to see, hear, smell, touch, or taste, nothing to feel or believe in.

In the following poem, Nan Fry's "The Plum," a sensory fascination with that plum (which may indeed have been sitting on the corner of her desk) leads the speaker into a complex web of emotion and thought. Notice that the concrete perceptions of the plum hold the web together, in fact weave it into a sort of bridge between poet and readers. The plum gives readers something to grasp, see, taste, and study, something far more enticing and intriguing than an earnest but simplistic commentary on "modern life," "instant gratification," or the ambiguities of pleasure.

Dark globe that fits easily into the palm,
your skin is speckled with pale galaxies,
an endless scattering.
Everywhere Adam and Eve are leaving
the Garden. You are the fruit we pluck
and eat. We need no serpent to urge us,
drawn as we are to your swelling,
your purple shading to rose, your skin
that yields to the touch, to the teeth:
all the world's waters and all its sweetness
rolled into fruit that explodes
on the tongue. We eat and drink flesh
the color of garnets, rubies, wounds.
It is bitter just under the skin.

When we return to our senses, then, we record in precise detail the circumstances that stimulated the emotion or provoked the opinion, the circumstances that resulted from it. Or if we are feeling particularly imaginative, we might try to embody that emotion or opinion in an invented *scene*. The scene may be completely "unrealistic"; yet we assemble it out of components derived from the senses, or *sensory images*. We rely on sensory images to reflect the inner state of heart or mind that we wish to express. In the following poem by James Tate, a series of surprising images describes the complicated paralysis suggested in the title.

Why I Will Not Get Out of Bed

My muscles unravel
like spools of ribbon:
there is not a shadow

of pain. I will pose
like this for the rest
of the afternoon,

for the remainder
of all noons. The rain
is making a valley

of my dim features.
I am in Albania,
I am on the Rhine.

It is autumn,
I smell the rain,
I see children running

through columbine.
I am honey,
I am several winds.

My nerves dissolve,
my limbs wither—
I don't love you.

I don't love you.

The images in Tate's poem jump around frantically, from now to forever and from here to Albania and the Rhine. Although the speaker's body languishes, his sensory life is alert: he imagines spools of ribbon in place of his muscles, as well as a valley where his "dim features" once appeared. He *smells* rain, he *is* honey, suggesting its taste and tactile quality. He *is* the turbulence of "several winds." This sensory activity underlines the urgency of the speaker's denial—first, of the "shadow of pain" and then, finally, of love—and betrays the intensity of his loss.

Speaking through the Senses

*Perception is unstable, its data shifting and subject to the inter-
play of the uncontrollable forces within our mind.*
                    Anton Ehrenzweig, *The Hidden Order of Art*

Speaking through the senses is expedient; it's good strategy. The
external, sensory world is what we have in common with our readers;
when we write about it, we stand a better chance of getting through to
them. This is not to suggest, though, that we typically begin with an idea
or a feeling and then deliberately sort through a repertory of sensory
images in order to embody it concretely. In fact, for example, it would be
surprising if Fry's poem started with something other than the cool, dark
weight of that plum.

Perception is never merely a matter of indiscriminately registering
what's going on "out there." What we perceive in the outer world is
influenced by our emotions, values, opinions—those issues that define
the inner world of the self. Indeed, it is through continuous interplay with
the outer world that the self takes shape and evolves. Each mirrors the
other; each influences the other in an endless loop. How we feel affects
what we see; what we see affects how we feel.

When the beginning writer mentioned earlier surveyed the items
on her desk, what sort of mood was she in? If she had felt more organized at that moment, if her perspective on life had been cheerier, might
she have noticed the photograph of her children, a birthday card from a
friend, a biology exam graded 94, a campaign button? In other words,
we may think we are merely gathering sensory information about the
world, but we are always also revealing and *discovering* the ideas and
feelings that comprise our selves. Despite their common contours, the
outer worlds that we must begin to explore are as different from each
other as we are.

EXERCISE: Observing Environment

Choose a place in your world that offers a lot of stimulation to the
senses. Make yourself comfortable there with your notebook, and for
fifteen minutes or so, record what you can see, hear, smell, touch, and
yes, taste. Notice that you can vary your distance from close-up to panorama. Concentrate on vividness and precision in your choice of words,
so that your reader will have the illusion of actually being there.

Read these records aloud to your class or group. What do the differences in location, focus, tone, and selection and sequence of detail suggest about the inner world of each writer, at least at the moment of writing? For each member's record, see if the group as a whole can agree on an abstract word or phrase that might identify the theme and serve as the title of the description.

You might wish to repeat this experiment with everyone writing in the same setting. Again, the amazing differences in results should reassure you: you are *always* expressing yourself, but self-expression is both more effective *and* more personally rewarding when you turn away from the self.

Opening the Senses

There are secrets everywhere, and everywhere revelations.
George Leonard, *The Silent Pulse*

Writers collect and cherish sensory images in much the same way that they treasure words, as the basic substance of their creative work. More fundamental than either genius or profound feeling is an alertness to the surrounding world, an ability to open the senses, to train them to catch all the details—subtle or obvious, sublime or ridiculous—that make up our lives.

This training means going against the "natural," survival function of the senses, which is not only to translate information from the outer world, but also to protect us from it. As physicists in this century have discovered, the "real" world consists of dynamic patterns of continuous energy waves pulsating at frequencies we can barely conceive of, much less witness. Waves of visible light, for example, pulse between 390 and 780 *trillion* times a second, yet specialized molecules in the cells of our retinas take in these dizzying, "invisible" rhythms and translate them into reassuring rainbows. The same sort of transmutations take place when we hear, smell, taste, or touch: special cells, barraged with an avalanche of stimuli, instantaneously, and for the most part mysteriously, fix this wave of possibilities with temporary shape and stability.

As awesome and intricate as the physiology of the senses may be, we must keep in mind their conservative, pragmatic tendencies. Their job is to zero in on sudden novelty that might threaten our survival, but once an event continues over time, they succumb all too readily to being lulled, even numbed, by simple routine. How else do we explain the parades of trite images brought to us by the media—the interchangeable living rooms of the sitcoms; the mountain lakes, tropical beaches, and sunsets; the cute babies, puppies, and kittens; and, of course, the uniformly sexy men and women?

As self-appointed guardians of business as usual, the unrocked boat, the low profile, the senses can hinder creative writing by slipping into lazy, uncreative perception. Writers have to fight against the tendency of the senses to take the familiar world for granted, and teach them instead to be *unnatural*, to risk indulging an obsessive appetite for all the world's details. Remember the popular image of the poet drifting down the street and maybe into the path of a truck because his or her head was in the clouds? Chances are it *wasn't* "in the clouds" at all but was simply preoccupied with taking in the infinite diversity of surrounding detail.

In her autobiography, *Mary*, Mary E. Mebane records in captivating detail her childhood memories of washing clothes outdoors in "a big iron pot that stood on three legs and was very black from soot." The process took all of Saturday to accomplish; the author's job was to "chunk" the clothes down in the pot, "dob" them around, and "jug" them from side to side with a large stick, as well as to "melt the bluing, which came in a long, flat cake," and skim the heavy translucent film from a smaller pot of flour-and-water starch. Finally, after dinner,

> the heavy things had boiled and Mama took them on a large stick to the washtub. The water in the tub was gray now with a high meringue of foam on it. But she rubbed and I rinsed, and she hung out the clothes high, but now she gave me the socks and sweaters to hang on the bushes. She sent me to see if any of the clothes were "hard," and I went to the line and lowered the stick that was holding it up. I took down the clothes that had been in the sun so long that they were dry and stiff.

Mebane's careful attention to sensory detail becomes reverential: she loved the slow, inevitable unfolding of these Saturdays, their natural rhythm. Creative, loving perception transforms a repetitive, monotonous chore into a precious ritual.

The less we take the familiar for granted, then, the more we revel in its familiarity—our intimate knowledge of the way it looks, smells, feels—the more we respect it enough to put it carefully into words, the more exotic it becomes. Such is the magical change the poet William Blake understood two hundred years ago when he asked, "How do you know but ev'ry Bird that cuts the airy way, / Is an immense world of delight, clos'd by your senses five?" Cleanse the "doors of perception," he urged, and "every thing would appear to man as it is, infinite."

EXERCISE: Recording a Meal

Make a list of foods—meats, fruits, sweets, and vegetables—you eat regularly. Choose one of your favorites from the list and imagine or recall a specific eating experience. How was the food prepared? Compose a detailed description, drawing on *all five* senses. Where was the food served, how, and by whom? Who was also present? What comments were made about this food? Describe any other foods present at the time in such a way that they will pale in comparison. Describe the one person you most associate with your food. Synthesizing the details you have recorded thus far, narrate a scene in which you are being served (or are serving yourself) this food and eating it. Try writing in the present tense.

Notice that close, affectionate attention to everyday reality can turn a routine repast into a banquet. Ask the members of your group which details of your meal seemed particularly arresting or "delightful."

• • •

Creative perception, then, discovers the extraordinary in the commonplace. Conversely, it also treats the extraordinary with the same sensory matter-of-factness as the everyday. (Imagine attending a banquet with royalty and writing about it as if it were Monday-night leftovers with your family.) In other words, if at a later stage you choose to write about the exotic—the fantastic or futuristic, the outrageous or zany—you must be careful not to lose your senses. Use as guides your descriptions of familiar settings from the preceding exercises, the dependability and consistency of their details, and push yourself to picture, hear, smell, taste, and touch the exotic in the same way. An invented setting should have the same immediacy and undeniability as a room you have slept in for the last five years. Such a setting establishes these primary claims through the senses. As its creator, you must be as familiar with its colors, shapes, sounds, odors, and textures as you are with the worlds in which you have worked and played.

Seeing Is Not Believing

Ours is a visual culture; for every adjective that describes the way an object sounds, smells, tastes, or feels, the English language offers dozens that describe the way it looks. And not surprisingly, because for every detail of sound, smell, taste, or touch we might notice about an object, we notice countless details about its appearance: shape, size, and color are only the most obvious. This sensory imbalance, this tyranny of the eye, is upheld by the media and poses a challenge to the writer determined to recreate a diversely concrete world in words.

Consider that the sense of sight permits the greatest distance between subject and object—light-years, in the case of the stars. Hearing requires more proximity, yet the sounds of explosions and jet engines can travel for miles. To smell something, we have to be much closer, in the same room with the object, perhaps; whereas taste and touch demand the physical contact that our civilized culture so often shies away from.

Given these differences, we can guess which sensory images we need to cultivate in order to create immediacy, to clinch concreteness in a world of words. In his autobiographical novel *Swann's Way,* the adult Marcel Proust takes a bite of a madeleine cake dipped in tea, and the *taste* plunges him back into the world of his childhood. How often has a *smell* such as after-shave or perfume, onion grass, engine oil, or horses brought vivid, emotional memories back to you? In fact, olfactory images wield a kind of primal power to evoke a substantial, irresistible world.

EXERCISE: A World of Scents

Imagine a culture in which smell rather than sight is the supreme sense. Make a list of the implications. What would happen to interior decoration, social patterns, plastic surgery, the media, entertainment? What would be considered a talent? a handicap? Would values change? You might put yourself in the paws of a dog you know and imagine what its interior life is like as a result of the tyranny of smell.

•   •   •

In her essay "A River's Route," Gretel Ehrlich recounts the stages of a quest through the Absaroka Mountains to find the source of a river. Just as this journey celebrates her passion for the wilderness, so the wild and surprising images of her essay jolt the senses out of their distant, civilized security and bring them smack up against the palpable earth.

> Last night I slept with my head butted against an Engelmann spruce, and on waking the limbs looked like hundreds of arms swinging in a circle. The trunk is bigger than an elephant's leg, bigger than my torso. I stick my nose against the bark. Tiny opals of sap stick to my cheeks and the bark breaks up, textured: red and gray, coarse and smooth, wet and flaked. . . . I eat baloney and cheese and . . . try to imagine what kinds of sweetness the earth provides: the taste of glacial flour, or the mineral taste of basalt, the fresh and foul bou-

quets of rivers, the desiccated, stinging flavor of a snowstorm—like eating red ants, my friend says.

As Ehrlich grapples with the insufficiencies of language to express things elemental and nonverbal, she verges on one strategy that writers often resort to: a sort of cross-referencing called *synesthesia,* in which a perception by one sense is expressed in terms of another. Ehrlich imagines herself eating the earth and heightens her already intense tactile under-standing of the wilderness with descriptions of taste. In an urban setting, snapping fingers might make a sharp, steel-blue sound, a beige might seem thick and slippery, or traffic noise might fade to a mute brown in the background. Experiment in your notebook with such hybridizing. You might, to begin with, choose a color and describe it using the senses other than sight. You might try specifically to render audiovisual images in terms of the more intimate, visceral smell, taste, and touch.

One reason to write is to create something original. That means using language energetically and precisely, avoiding ready-made phrases or clichés, words that have been used and abused to death. Powerful creative writing demands alertness and accuracy in sensory perception as well as in the use of language. If you learn to express yourself through sensory images, to perceive the everyday world more inclusively, more creatively, to discover its distinctive, delightful details, this respect for sensory detail will stay with you when you remember and dream.

NOTEBOOK OPTIONS

1. Begin a collection of sensory images, listing them by category. Do visual images come abundantly to you, outstripping the other senses? When you try to pay closer attention to smell, taste, and touch—the contact senses—do you find the language letting you down? In the absence of words for perceived qualities, what do you do?

    A physiologist will tell us, for example, that our taste palette offers a mere four options: sweet, sour, salty, and bitter. Yet how many different "shades" of each taste can you list? Notice that you must resort to *naming things* that taste: *honey-sweet* versus *molasses-sweet; mango-sweet* versus *grape-sweet.* The physiologist would contend that these shades are more a matter of smell than taste, but that disclaimer doesn't help us put them into words.

2. Contemplate a familiar object (a key, a banana, a hockey puck, a matchbook) until you have composed five observations about it for each of the five senses. Feel free to fiddle with your object both

physically and imaginatively. Drop it from varying heights; picture it in different contexts.

3. Make a list of purple things (or purple parts of things). Weave them into a paragraph of description or narration.

4. There are as many different kinds of *soft* as there are soft things. Make lists of things noted for their softness, their roughness, their elasticity, their stickiness, their crispness. Think of these as a reservoir of things you can name—comparisons you can make—when you are trying to capture texture.

5. When we think of perception, we tend to think of persons, places, and things and their qualities. We need to remind ourselves that we also perceive *actions* by means of sight, hearing, and even touch. To strengthen your ability to describe a variety of particular actions accurately and concretely, begin keeping lists of energetic or unusual verbs. Here are some possible categories:

> verbs having to do with a particular sport (besides the familiar baseball and football, consider the rich terminology of sports like fencing, figure skating, tennis)
> verbs having to do with the preparation of food
> verbs having to do with eating and digestion
> verbs for all the different ways sounds can come out of the mouth
> verbs for all the different ways a human being can move the body from one point to another

As you add new verbs to your lists, be sure that you associate each one with a distinct sensory picture. Try to appreciate how simmering is different from boiling, parrying from blocking, muttering from whispering.

6. Make a list of the most predictable, superficial, and sentimental scenes or situations that the media too frequently bring us. Include both the familiar and the exotic—the common thread will be the "generic" quality of their images: the fiery sunsets of the Caribbean; the perfect, happy, wartless, zitless family next door; the addict who kicks the habit in ten minutes; the puppy who munches kibbles and looks cute; the prostitute who never contracts AIDS and marries for love. Choose one scene or situation and bring some part of it to life by imagining it as specifically as you can with all five of your senses. In other words, pay meticulous attention to one particular sunset, kitten, mom in a kitchen, or drug user.

7. Make a list of places or situations that you associate with unusual and/

or intense sounds. Compose a brief description of one noisy place using only words associated with the other four senses.

8. Imagine one of the following radically unfamiliar "worlds:"

> a tropical rainforest
> a mountain monastery in a distant land
> a village within the Arctic circle
> a U.S. city one hundred years from now
> an undiscovered planet

If you prefer, come up with a setting on your own, building on any bits of knowledge you may have about history, geography, or science. In either case, study your created world with each of the five senses, jotting down details as they come to mind, from the obvious to the wild guess. Initially, your images may seem generic, or predictable. Without firsthand experience of your world, you must create your world out of other images you may have gathered from reading, movies, or the media. However, once you have sketched the general outlines, let your senses guess at more specific details. Don't worry about plausibility or "realism," just sensory concreteness. Many of the details of your own "real life" might be judged as implausible when closely examined.

9. Focus your full range of perceptual attention on a fellow human being whom you find attractive, using discretion, obviously, where the contact senses are concerned. The challenge here is to avoid the overused generic qualities and images (blond hair, blue eyes; tall, dark, and handsome) purveyed by our culture. In describing visual appearance, in particular, strive for the distinctive, unexpected details.

10. Imagine that you are carrying a camera, still or movie, as you go about your daily activities and that you are looking for interesting—pleasing or meaningful—shots or scenes. Take some time to jot down one or two.

Chapter 4

Remembering

The charm, one might say the genius, of memory is that it is choosy, chancy and temperamental; it rejects the edifying cathedral and indelibly photographs the small boy outside, chewing a hunk of melon in the dust.

Elizabeth Bowen, *Vogue*

William Wordsworth famously defines poetry as "emotion recollected in tranquillity." This phrase announces a truly modern poetry, a poetry that begins in the individual, refers to individual experiences, and weds the present with the past in universal ways. For Wordsworth, modern writers understand themselves as cut off from a past they can recover only by an energetic willed act of *remembering*. And through this act of remembering they see both their uniqueness (they record, after all, "their own" memories) and their universality.

The Act of Remembering As an Act of Creating

The act of remembering is not simply a process of recording past events and perceptions, however; the act of remembering is an act of creation. We experience the present within the shadows of the past, according to Wordsworth, and we recollect (re-collect) our impressions of the past from the perspective of the present, a perspective that constantly changes. In other words, present experiences are always colored or influenced by the past, and the past is reviewed through the lens of the present. We remember certain images and events when we're depressed and others when we're happy, and we understand the same past event in different ways at different times in our lives. For Wordsworth, every act of

33

cognition is, in a strong sense, an act of memory, and every act of memory is, in an even stronger sense, potentially a poem. Through memory, we compose the past.

In remembering, the writer revisits a scene, reconstructing the sensory details on which emotion hangs its coat. Note the sights and sounds that introduce Wordsworth's "Lines Composed a Few Miles above Tintern Abbey":

> Five years have passed; five summers, with the length
> Of five long winters! and again I hear
> These waters, rolling from their mountain-springs
> With a soft inland murmur. Once again
> Do I behold these steep and lofty cliffs. . . .
>   Once again I see
> These hedgerows, hardly hedgerows, little lines
> Of sportive wood run wild; these pastoral farms,
> Green to the very door; and wreaths of smoke
> Sent up, in silence, from among the trees!

EXERCISE: Recalling a Place

Recall a place from your childhood, a place more particular and limited than Cleveland, Ohio or out west. List five things you remember seeing there, including as many details about these things as you can. In other words, don't merely list "swingset, path, and white apartments," but shade them in a bit: "the sturdy metal swingset my father had made," "the wide path that narrowed as it approached the thicker woods," and "the clapboard white apartment houses, each of which housed six families."

Reaching for the same specificity, train your other senses on this childhood place and create the following lists: the sounds (both natural and unnatural) and bits of conversation you heard there; the textures you associate with this place (for example, the cold metal railing, the smooth plaster walls, your mother's slippery jersey dress); the smells you associate with the place; and the tastes you recall. Using the details from your lists, write a description of this place. Think about the choices available for the structure of your description. It can flow as linear narrative ("I did _____, then _____, and finally _____"); it can move from the whole to the part, from panorama to close-up; or it can travel in the opposite direction, from particular detail to the larger context.

•   •   •

Because we know our own lives better than anyone else's and better than any character's we might invent, we can tap this reservoir with ease. Even a single word can stimulate a chain of recollections. Consider the scene or cluster of scenes you associate with each of the following: *swing, basement, kiss, gym, hide.* Each scene plays vividly in our minds. As writers, we seek to retrieve that past impression and reconstitute it on the page, forceful and stunning in its new context. Often, however, we only manage to suggest the shadowy outlines of the original; we obscure a powerful memory by overexplaining it, by telling rather than showing. Rather than describing Bobby Wilson, the pimply star forward we watched make the final tie-breaking lay-up of the season, we might in a first draft (of a poem, story, or personal essay) talk generally about sports in our high school or about how we felt bad about never making the varsity team.

Remember that writing from memory requires probing the scene for details on which the scene's effect will turn. No paragraph discussing the importance of high-school sports ever made a story about the championship basketball game come alive. To bring it to life, you have to transport the reader from the complacency of the present into the stands of the overheated, overlighted high-school gym where the center, Bobby Wilson, rises through the sweat and with long, firm arms dunks the ball through the hoop, and where the sophomore girl you don't even know sitting behind you in the stands leaps up and hugs you, and where the blessing of winning falls on the whole school for that instant.

In writing about any setting, character, or event from your past, keep in mind that there are many choices available to you. You can enhance or exaggerate certain aspects: the threads in the carpet or the messiness of a nightstand, a simple gesture or an irksome habit, the care with which your grandfather baited his hooks, or the roughness of a kiss. You can speak from the first- or third-person point of view, describe the event from your mother's perspective (or from your brother's or a friend's). You can highlight contrasts or draw analogies. You make some of these choices without being fully aware that you have made them, without having considered the alternatives. But in even the simplest, most preliminary draft, you tentatively, at least, chart a direction.

Take a look at the accounts below, each describing a visit to an elderly aunt in a nursing home. Trace the structure of each passage and decide what choices the writer has made in each selection:

1. I entered the Gillette Home through the aluminum storm door with the cursive silver G in the center, into the dimly lit wood-paneled foyer and up the noisy walnut stairs to the stale second floor. As I made my way down the linoleum hallway (its twisting

gray paisley worn in the center), an old man raised his thin, white-robed arm and called to me, but I didn't stop, not till I came to the overheated yellow bedroom in the back where my Aunt Jose sat in the small rocker near her bed with the smooth, too-white spread.

2. Across the tracks, the white Victorian quietly rested at the end of the street. It maintained a shabby elegance and an uneasy serenity on the outskirts of this small upstate farming town. The ambulatory patients clustered in threes and fours on the glassed-in porch; the others either lay in their upstairs single beds or sat in rockers beside them. Two or three times a week I'd sit with my aunt and play dominoes or pinochle on the green vinyl card table.

3. "Oh, no you little stinker you; you beat me again!" she'd always shout as she leaned her thin body back from the green card table. Her anger at me was as feigned as my innocence. Even at eight I knew that she'd let me win, but I never let on. That was the real game we played.

4. Mom always insisted that my sister visit Aunt Jose at the nursing home on holidays, despite my sister's obvious distaste for such mandatory courtesy. She said the place smelled, and besides, she had plans for the day. But I rather liked going—not so much on the obligatory holiday visits but on my own. I'd walk over a couple days a week and play games with my aunt. Lots of times she'd let me win. I remember those summer afternoons fondly. Time seemed to stand still.

Each of these paragraphs is written from a first-person point of view, yet each defines a different focus. How do these paragraphs introduce us to the nursing home? to its inhabitants? to their visitors? What possibilities for further development does each open up? What possibilities does each foreclose? If you were filming this nursing home, which of these paragraphs would be most useful to you? How would you film it: long shots, close-ups, tracking shot, or voice-over? Look at the scene you described in the preceding exercise, and ask yourself the same question.

Taking License with the Past

In translating life into art, you can take some license. Your grandfather's tie might be a little bolder, the bed a little lumpier, the chair a different color Naugahyde, or the service a little slower. The dialogue of a family quarrel might contain bits of conversation exchanged in several disputes. The traits of several individuals might be collapsed into one.

Whereas a particular episode may, in fact, have involved ten family members, you may choose to populate your story with only two or three because you can't possibly develop those ten as individuals distinct from one another.

EXERCISE: The Composite Character

Recall two childhood or teenage friends of the same gender, and write two lists, one that describes one friend and another that describes the other. Include in your lists details of both how they looked and how they behaved. Aim for ten observations in each list. One friend might have been stubborn, a collector of coins, and someone who could outrun anyone else in the class. The other might have embarrassed you once with her loudness, come from a home with a peculiar mother, and always had her hand up in class.

Now write a description of a "composite" friend by including a few items from each list. Feel free to give yourself a little license here to move beyond the literal "truth." Let your composite character come to life by demanding new and independent traits of his or her own.

Familiarity

Writing from memory carries with it its own difficulties. Familiarity can curse as well as bless us. When we write from memory, we know our characters, their actions, and their haunts so well that we sometimes unfairly assume the same level of intimacy on the part of our readers. We often take our readers for granted by casting characters adrift as little more than ghostly shadows of themselves. In working from memory, we often cut swiftly to the bare facts, forgetting to include the details that restore life to the scene.

Take, for example, the student who wrote about her cousin LaVonne's adventure in the Masonic temple:

> My cousin, LaVonne, was three years older than me. My mother always said that even as a little child LaVonne was "full of the devil." But I sort of liked LaVonne and secretly admired her when I heard how she had snuck into the Masonic temple a few blocks from her house the night they had their secret initiation. Unfortunately, she got caught trying to sneak out. They called her mother, and LaVonne had all hell to pay.

Both LaVonne and her exploits make excellent subjects for a story, but this writer has reduced LaVonne to a simple generalization (she was "full of the devil") and her adventure to the kernel of a story (she snuck in and got caught sneaking out, incurring the wrath of her mother). The writer needs to open this up with more information about LaVonne's childhood. What did LaVonne do even as a little kid to deserve her reputation? The writer clearly appreciates LaVonne's boldness more than either of their mothers does; she needs to exploit this tension, revealing more of what she knows about LaVonne: how she walks, how she snaps her gum in front of adults, the rings she wears, her outlandish outfits and loud lipstick, and the stern looks she elicits from her mother.

The writer should begin by reminding herself of all she knows about LaVonne and her adventures, all the time taking copious notes on such details. But at some point, she'll want to step back and see not only who LaVonne is but what she could become in the story. This is the point at which remembering slips into invention, where fact and fiction work hand in hand as the writer pieces together what has existed in her own past with what she brings into existence in the world of her fiction. She moves beyond the simple record of her past; she makes a piece of art.

In this way, creative writing is different from diary writing. Although the raw material we mold may be the result of reflections on lived experiences, we generally seek to construct something apart from ourselves through such reflection: a piece of art with its own cohesion and form, something with beauty and significance beyond disclosure.

Diaries have keys for a reason; they hold secrets the writer wishes to record but not disclose to others. Diarists record thoughts and feelings but rarely include any of the data of their experiences:

> Nothing seemed to go right today. When I woke up I felt ok, but then I was late for class. I had done the wrong history assignment, and I nodded off in math. I can't wait for vacation. I can't wait to get back home, to have a little rest from this pressure.

In writing creatively, we may confess secrets, but we assume that we are going public with them, at least as public as the classroom. We take a longer perspective than the glance over the day's activities typical of the diary. We gain some consciousness of craft; we keep in mind both what we have to tell and how we tell it.

In the following poem, notice how Geraldine Connolly tells us about three old women through their actions, their clothing, their possessions, their faces, and their gifts.

Godmothers

I wanted them to come from God,
but they were orphans Mother said
slowing the word so deliciously

it almost stuck to the roof
of her mouth. We called them "aunt,"
Ann, Eve, Flo—water syllables.

When they played pinochle
with the real aunts and uncles,
they stuck out like garden markers.

The Rendulich sisters, childless,
straightbacked at the oak table;
no fairy tale could have contained them,

bony and gaunt, thumbing
their cards, then touching
a fingertip to their tongues.

Each had her own illness,
complicated and distinct
as their mosaic pillboxes.

Faces flushed with nicotine and rouge,
they picked out colored pills
from silver compartments precisely

on the hour. We loved our evenings
with them, flavored by horehound drops
and whispers of the doctor's critical visit.

Their sweater clips were clipped shut
beneath stern jabots. A crystal
paperweight one of them

stiffly presented me once
held hickory leaves, trapped
and dry inside its glacier.

Making Use of Collective Memory

Every family maintains a repertory of family stories: accounts of courtship and marriage, of coming to America or moving to another part of the country, of fortunes won and lost, of traditional names and nick-names, of hard times, of uncanny moments, and of infamous family char-acters. These stories, along with the colorful sayings and peculiar expres-sions of families and their manner of observing holidays and other rituals (birthdays, funerals, and so on), constitute family folklore. This reservoir of stories (often begun with fact and embellished with fiction) runs deep and wide in many families and offers the writer a rich source of creative material.

Recall the stories (or bits of stories) your parents, grandparents, aunts, and uncles have recounted to you. What do such accounts tell you about your family? What do they celebrate? What do they caution against? Remember not just the facts of these stories but also the ways in which they were told. Did the teller ever gesture elaborately or pepper accounts with flavorful expressions? Was the weather always "colder than a well digger's butt" or the coffee so strong "it nearly bent the spoon"? Did the listeners delight in the colorful speech as much as in the unfolding of misadventures? Were some listeners indifferent or bored by such stories?

EXERCISE: Family Stories

Retell a family story. The story may have as its focus either an event that happened before your time or one you witnessed yourself. To prime your memory, consider accounts of the following:

> pranks
> home remedies
> unusual dates, jilted brides, elopements, arranged marriages
> the effect of a war on your family
> unusual names and nicknames
> family eccentrics
> black sheep
> precious objects
> times of family crisis
> advice
> the origin of a family tradition
> discipline

Imagine yourself to be the storyteller who embellishes the slim plot of an event with full descriptions of place and character. Consider dialogue as a way of bringing characters to life. Breathe enough life into your characters so that they appear real to a reader who does not share your memories or your background.

·   ·   ·

Just as every family breeds at least one black sheep, every town or neighborhood sports at least one eccentric. Whether the hills of Tennessee or the streets of Philadelphia, every region has its own tales and its own way of telling. Recall those stories and catch the flavor of that way of talking, and you'll furnish a richer environment for your characters. Stick with what you know; don't mimic the "folksiness" of a group you haven't lived among. Your results will ring as phony as canned laughter or as out of place as cowboy boots on a Bostonian.

Whether you exploit your collective or your personal memory, you'll discover recollections a rich starting place for poems, stories, or personal essays. In the following passage from "Three Women: Cultural Rules and Leadership Roles in the Black Community," Jacquelyn Mitchell recalls Ma, her maternal grandmother who spent her days holding court from her front stoop:

> She sat each day on the stoop like an ageless queen granting a royal audience to an endless parade of city diplomats. There were the winos, the muttering street poets, the junkie socialites, and the sanctified tambourine-playing church members on their way to daily prayer meeting. The clanging staccato rhythm made by the "door-key" kids clinking beer cans against curbs punctuated the beat of the quartet of local street dudes harmonizing Frankie Lymon and the Teenagers' latest hit. Tired women, mothers laden with shopping bags heavy with the week's groceries, rushed to cook and clean again, having cleaned the white folks' homes all day. And gangling me with knees sidewalk-battered, face pumpkin-round, pensive, sitting silently, watching Ma's unending receiving line. Each morning around nine, her throne—a padded, yellow, vinyl and chrome chair—was positioned on the same strategic lookout stoop, and returned to the kitchen when the fireflies signaled her bedtime.

Interestingly, as the specific details of this description accumulate, personal memory grows larger-than-life; the particular becomes universal. Ma acquires the stature of an "ageless queen." The carefully rendered population of her neighborhood define a whole microcosmic world.

NOTEBOOK OPTIONS

1. Pick someone from your childhood whom you did not particularly enjoy being with (someone you might even call a childhood enemy), and recall a single scene involving this person.

   • Describe this individual, yourself, and anyone else gathered in this scene.
   • Write a letter to this person in which you describe this scene and indicate its importance through the details you select. Remember to show, not tell.

2. Write down as many details as you can about a relative whom you view as peculiar or eccentric in some way. Write a description of this relative from those details and from others that occur to you, a description that reveals rather than states how you (or you and other family members) regard this relative.

3. Make a list of the ten memories you would not want to part with. Make a list of the ten memories you would gladly be rid of.

4. Write about a childhood experience in which you witnessed the vulnerability of an adult—for example, a time when you saw an adult hurt, overwhelmed, or caught in a lie.

5. Recall a time when, as a teenager or preteen, you felt vulnerable. Describe that time without using any words that *explain* how you felt. In other words, strive to convince your reader that you were lonely, sad, frightened, whatever, without mentioning any of these abstract words.

6. Remember the cutup, the class clown, the flunky, or the outcast in grade school or high school. Write a description of one such person, including specific examples of this person's exploits. As you write, reflect on the attitudes of others towards this person: other students, teachers, the principal.

Chapter 5

Dreaming Awake

Dreams, dreams, dreams, all is but a dream where the wind wanders, and the barking dogs come out on the roads.
André Breton, "The Manifesto of Surrealism"

Creative writers make believe. They train themselves sharply to observe the world around them, to notice the unnoticed. They reach back into their past lives for rich characters, vivid settings, and meaningful events. But at some point, the search for raw material veers toward another source—it turns inward to what isn't, wasn't, and could never be, yet somehow seems right, real, and true.

Dream Thought

Like the preceding chapters on sensory perception and remembering, this chapter focuses on a familiar mental process as a way of generating material for creative writing. Though some of us may retain only fragmentary evidence, we generate material every night in our dreams.

Dreams create a private world unrestrained by the rules that govern the waking world: one person suddenly turns into another, time races and then creeps, gravity loosens its chains, people die and come back to life. Dreams combine the people, places, and events from everyday lives, past and present, according to a mysterious, intuitive logic. Though we often can't claim to understand what a dream means, we can sense that it is meaningful.

The universality of dreaming is reassuring proof of the natural and spontaneous creativity of the human mind. As writers, we must learn how to tap into that creativity and draw some of its energy under our more

43

conscious control. Sigmund Freud, one of the first to analyze dreams scientifically, identified a number of characteristics of *dream thought:*

1. It relies on images rather than words.
2. It connects and combines these images by free association.
3. It isn't bothered in the least by contradiction.
4. It breaks free of Newtonian notions of space and time.
5. It isn't embarrassed by impropriety.

He labeled dream thought "primary process thinking" and distinguished it from "secondary process thinking," which sticks to all the rules—of logic, of grammar, of science, and of society. Primary process thinking, Freud suggested, is the process that governs our thinking in early childhood, before our education into Western scientific culture teaches us to outgrow it. We revert to it in our dreams when our educated conscious minds are asleep.

As Freud's beneficiaries, willing or not, contemporary writers have discovered that this deeper, more primitive kind of thinking has the potential for great resonance. Everyone has engaged in it, though many claim to forget that they have, just as they claim to forget their dreams and much of their childhood. In the following poem, "Eating Poetry," Mark Strand displays proudly and playfully the various inventions of primary process thinking. See if you can point them out.

Ink runs from the corners of my mouth.
There is no happiness like mine.
I have been eating poetry.

The librarian does not believe what she sees.
Her eyes are sad
and she walks with her hands in her dress.

The poems are gone.
The light is dim.
The dogs are on the basement stairs and coming up.

Their eyeballs roll,
their blond legs burn like brush.
The poor librarian begins to stamp her feet and weep.

She does not understand.
When I get on my knees and lick her hand,
she screams.

I am a new man.
I snarl at her and bark.
I romp with joy in the bookish dark.

Mad dogs lunge suddenly from a library basement to shake the authority of a repressed librarian. An old metaphor (to read a book is to consume and digest it) is taken literally and shown concretely. The reader/poet is transformed into a joyous dog. Images shift abruptly and without explanation. Such is the stuff of dreams; yet clearly, dream thought did not spontaneously produce this poem. Freud's model of adult mental processes proposes *two* distinct activities; so does our model of the writing process. Whereas in the first phase of freewriting, list making, and brainstorming we indulge primary process impulses freely and fully, we always contain them in the second phase, in which we select, shape, and question. It seldom serves aesthetic purposes to recreate in full the bizarre originality of a dream. Yet it is often useful to tap into dreams in smaller ways—for unusual images or surprising twists in character and plot.

EXERCISE: Dream Logic

To practice certain aspects of "dreaming" deliberately, you need to suspend the rules governing "realistic" writing and adopt an associative or dream logic. Even if this sort of play does not lead to a finished piece of writing, it will flex your imagination and widen your frame of reference to include the unpredictable and even the impossible.

Make a list of twenty strong action verbs. You might consider verbs associated with play or sport, food or eating, locomotion, plant life. Next make separate lists of objects—some small and some large; of parts of objects—the bristles on a brush, the keys on a typewriter; and of specific places intimately familiar to you.

Following impulse and intuition rather than reason, choose two or three words or images you like from each list, and arrange an interesting sentence around them. Try this five or six times, taking chances on unusual combinations. Imagine, for example, light leaking from a 100-watt bulb, a washer taking root in the corner of a messy cellar, or smooth keys kicking at the pianist's touch. You will certainly produce sentences that seem silly, but you will undoubtedly generate several interesting images. Finally, allow your most fertile sentence(s) to spin a descriptive paragraph that details a dream landscape or an unusual experience.

Surrealism

The real and the dream became one, or rather reality was one of the dream's configurations.

Jorge Luis Borges, "Parable of the Palace"

A group of writers and artists working in the 1920s and 1930s sought deliberately to suspend their art between the world of dream and the world of reality. At the points of confrontation between these opposites (reason and irrationality), the group claimed to discover a special reality, a "surreality." Along that margin, the Surrealists hoped, language would be liberated from the rationality that imprisoned it and transformed into shockingly vibrant imagery that would force us to question the staid everyday world through which we blindly pass.

Contradiction pulses at the heart of surrealist imagery. Snow falls upward and the rain bites in the poems of Tristan Tzara; a red fish descends through a barn roof in Benjamin Peret's "La Brébis Galante"; the world turns "blue like an orange" in work by Paul Eluard.

EXERCISE: Capturing Unreality

In notebook option 2 in Chapter 3: Coming to Our Senses, you were invited to contemplate a familiar object and write down your sensory impressions of it. In this exercise, you may resurrect that object or choose to explore something new with your five senses, making a list of its various characteristics. When you feel you have enough realistic notes on the object, compose a description of it that runs *counter* to its real nature. Begin this description by placing the object in a setting least likely to contain it.

For example, here is a list of adjectives we might use to describe a pen: *shiny, thin, smooth, pointed,* and *black and white.* To employ these pedestrian adjectives to describe a pen might make the writing precise, but it wouldn't make it particularly interesting. But let us abandon for a moment the logic of everyday associations and choose instead the opposites of those adjectives: *rough, dull, fat, blunt,* and *orange.* We might then write something like the following:

> Some days the pen is too rough to hold. Dull and fat, it scrapes at my hand, and produces nothing I'd choose to remember. After a night of jerky scribbling, I plant its blunt orange body among the hollyhocks.

Describing an object by using words not typically associated with it, we, in effect, free it from the complex net of assumptions that so often limit its possibilities and imprison its predictability.

•   •   •

Writers other than Surrealists also embrace an antilogical approach to composition in order to invite the unusual, the spontaneous, and the accidental. Whether or not you recall actual dreams, you can indulge in dream thinking at different stages in the writing process. Perhaps a character in a story seems a little dull. Compile a list of adjectives describing him or her, then flip these traits into their opposites to uncover productive contradictions. Or suppose a setting seems lifeless and merely obligatory. Try listing items that couldn't be found in it, and then including one. Although such experiments may sometimes produce the ridiculous, risking the ridiculous allows for the possibility of the truly original.

EXERCISE: An Imaginary City

There are several parts of this assignment. It is important that you do them in order.

1. Limiting yourself to only ten minutes, write a general paragraph or two describing the daily lives of the residents of any U.S. city. Don't try to be clever; this is just a matter-of-fact outline of the lives of the inhabitants of Pittsburgh or Paducah, of Boise or Binghamton.

2. Select one of the following adjectives, and make a list of five to ten words you associate with your adjective. The word *liquid*, for example, might produce a list including verbs that describe the actions of a liquid substance (*wiggle, flow, stream, spill,* and *pour*), related adjectives (*wet, clear, murky, smooth*), as well as nouns associated with things liquid (*oceans, cups, oil, coffee,* even *lava lamps*).

sharp	luminous	muscular
glass	gaseous	soft
hard	rubber	bony
velvet	woven	plastic

3. In this step, describe an imaginary city that displays the adjective you selected in step 2. Just start writing about whatever details come to mind. When you find yourself pausing, consult your

realistic paragraph(s) or the following list for additional things you might describe:

the city's geographic location
its history
its weather
its natural resources
what the city produces and the kinds of work its people do
where people live
how they spend their leisure time
how they are governed
their beliefs and rituals
whether there are differences among the inhabitants
its youth (if there are any) and their education
the city's final moments in time

The brief description of a liquid city that follows may suggest some possibilities. Remember that you need not bind yourself to the rules that govern the real world. Imaginary places pulse and spin to their own natural laws.

On a bad day, the place is a dull green bile color. People slowly pour themselves into their clothing and slosh to work. At the factory, they spill down the glass sides of filmy hallways, deep into the basement. At the end of their murky day, the factory is lifted and tilted by long straps till the workers splash past one another through the long rush hour streams. On weekends, the liquid city clears, so transparent that people can see in and through each other. Everyone rises late from the small individual cups of their watery sleep.

•   •   •

The preceding exercise was inspired by Italo Calvino's imaginatively rich descriptive detail in *Invisible Cities*. When the explorer Marco Polo returns from his incredible journeys, he entertains the Emperor Kubla Khan with tales of his travels to lushly detailed cities of the mind. Octavia, the spider-web city, is one such place.

Now I will tell how Octavia, the spider-web city, is made. There is a precipice between two steep mountains: the city is over the void, bound to the two crests with ropes and chains and catwalks. You walk on the little wooden ties, careful not to set your foot in the open spaces, or you cling to the hempen strands. Below there is nothing for hundreds and hundreds of feet: a few clouds glide past; farther down you can glimpse the chasm's bed.

This is the foundation of the city: a net which serves as passage and as support. All the rest, instead of rising up, is hung below: rope ladders, hammocks, houses made like sacks, clothes hangers, terraces like gondolas, skins of water, gas jets, spits, baskets on strings, dumb-waiters, showers, trapezes and rings for children's games, cable cars, chandeliers, pots with trailing plants.

Suspended over the abyss, the life of Octavia's inhabitants is less uncertain than in other cities. They know the net will last only so long.

Note the movement of this description from the whole to its parts— from the city's spider-web architecture to the objects suspended from the net—and, finally, to inhabitants who know "the net will last only so long." Notice too how lists, Calvino's long chains of details, can actually become part of a finished piece of writing. Try this technique in your own description.

In additional writing about your city, you might choose to focus on one inhabitant (an ordinary Joe or Jane) of this city and describe him or her, or to compose the text of a travel brochure designed to induce people from other cities to take advantage of everything your city has to offer.

Obviously, in writing such fantasy the writer abandons certain scientific rules governing the rational world but maintains others. To be comprehensible, the extraordinary must relate in some way to the ordinary. In Calvino's impossible city, the inhabitants cook their food, store their water, take showers, and their children play—mundane activities that in the unusual landscape of the imaginary city take on a peculiar fascination. Calvino delicately suspends the net of his prose between the possible and the impossible, leaving the reader poised, rapt for a moment in wonder.

The Dangers of Dreaming

Dream thinking as one source of creative writing must be approached with some caution. If you have already read aloud to your classmates the results of some of these exercises, you may have noticed that a piece of your writing you thought was wonderful received only lukewarm praise as well as directions, perhaps, for further work. Incorporating dreaming into creative writing is tricky business. For while fantasy material may be highly original, and fascinating to you, it may also be so personal that it makes no sense to anyone else. Consider, for example, how you react when an acquaintance announces, "Hey, I had the wildest dream last night; let me tell you about it," and proceeds to recount the narrative detail by detail. You might stay interested for the first couple of "wild" happenings, but pretty soon, their very wildness, the absence of a familiar logic, becomes monotonous, and you begin to think of ways to make your escape.

When you write, your ultimate purpose is to touch and move your audience, not to drive them away. Keep in mind that dream thinking is only a means to literary art, not the end in itself. It can provide wonderful raw material. As you work with it, however, weigh seriously the feedback that comes to you from fellow writers. In the early stages of writing, in the process of developing a critical ear, outside guidance can help you decide what to select, when to condense or amplify—how to create meaningful sequences.

If creative writing thrives on "dreaming," risking the ridiculous in hope of discovering the stunning moment, image, or phrase, it also requires "waking," taking a second look and raising questions about purpose and effect.

NOTEBOOK OPTIONS

1. Make a list of five actions you would likely observe in the library (people reading books, taking notes, and so on). Now make a second list of ten things you would not be likely to see in the library. Almost anything may find its way onto this list: a mother kissing her son goodbye, a snake slithering, someone firing an M-16, or a woman in gold evening gown doing the tango with a man in tails. Write a narrative about your visit to a library where a selection of these activities were going on.

2. Imagine for a moment that your mind changed shape with your moods. Would sloth make it limp, jellylike, weak, and useless? Would anger splinter it into a thousand glaring shards? When would it be pond-flat and still? Select three moods, and describe the shape your mind might assume with each mood.

3. Make the following lists: adjectives that might describe a landscape; things noted for their texture; occupations. Next assign the adjectives to the people (occupations) you've listed, and let each person do something with an object. You'll generate some interesting and some totally ridiculous combinations. Ignore the silly ones, and select as the focus of a descriptive paragraph one of the combinations that works.

4. Make a list of ten small places, nothing as vast as a train station, places more modest in size: a bed, a desk drawer, the inside of an avocado, a

cereal bowl. Next introduce into these places objects that you would be unlikely to find there. Don't think very long about this, just jot down the objects that come randomly to mind:

> the red flower blooming in a desk drawer
> the bones in the cereal bowl
> the ring inside the orange

If you haven't added any adjectives to your list, go back and do so (for example, the tan bones in the white cereal bowl). Then write a paragraph or so around one of these images.

5. Make a list of objects that we always pair: peanut butter and jelly, knife and fork, field and stream. Choose one of these "odd couples" and record a conversation between them. What might they argue about?

6. Beginning with the conventional "Once upon a time . . . ," freewrite a fairy tale, allowing yourself no more time to consider what you are setting down than the pace of your handwriting or typing dictates. Try to let a picture emerge and evolve in your mind as you record whatever details come into focus. If you seem to want to write off on a tangent of description, narration, or characterization, don't resist; go with the flow.

PART TWO

Exploring Technique

Chapter 6

Focusing Tension

Poetry is a theorem of a yellow-silk handkerchief knotted with riddles, sealed in a balloon tied to the tail of a kite flying in a white wind against a blue sky.
Carl Sandburg, "Ten Definitions of Poetry"

Creative writers are drawn by what the poet William Butler Yeats called "the fascination of what's difficult." What is creative writing itself but an heroic attempt at the impossible—the translation of concrete life into abstract words without any losses? In addition, the very techniques that purport to bolster the process seem only to make it harder. As later chapters will explore, powerful writing requires precise images instead of general commentary; it weaves connections among things as diverse as hyacinths and biscuits and evolves from odd angles of vision recounted in distinctive voices. It may disrupt chronological order; it may reinvent logical order; it may interrupt sentences, even individual words, with poetic line breaks. Creative writers are forever stringing a tightwire from their first word to their last and trying a daring dance between.

Tension is enhanced by "technique," the various ingenious ways of working with material. But what about the raw material itself? In powerful writing, tension must reside in its deeper levels as well. Whereas later chapters will introduce various technical principles to begin developing and shaping a piece of writing, this chapter addresses more basic questions: As you scan your exercises and freewriting with the idea of creating a finished product, what should you be looking for? How will you recognize the pregnant subject when it presents itself? Perhaps your intuition about subject matter is already strong—you know you *have* to write about a certain character or place. How do you begin to focus its possibilities?

55

The Tension of Doubt

The early stages of creative writing are rarely accompanied by certainty. Passion maybe, compulsion maybe, momentary visions of enticing clarity maybe, but certainty—that we have come to the right forest and are following the right track—not often. Even when we feel we *have* to write about a particular subject, clouds of doubt often gather around it as soon as we begin to consider it seriously for further work.

In the case of this book, you may be having difficulty seeing a connection between the writing you have come up with in response to exercises and the perfect, polished product, "what you had in mind" before you opened it. Some of the exercises may seem gimmicky, contrived; you may be wondering whether the writing they induced is really "you."

All these doubts are natural, part of the creative process, which after all requires us to rely on intuition, follow wild ideas, play hunches, let go of conscious control. "Creative work," suggests the psychologist and art historian Anton Ehrenzweig, is "done in interim stages involving interim decisions," and the artist "has to forego the wish to visualize precisely the final appearance of his work." In other words, once we have generated some promising fragments, we must bear with the *tension of not knowing*, consciously and exactly, how our imaginations will manage to fill in gaps and create coherence.

The creative process can be frustrating and confusing; it *is* disorganized, compared to composing a research paper from notecards and an outline. What it takes at this intermediate stage is faith—faith that a number of "right" subjects are ready and waiting in rough form in your notebook—maybe implicit in this brief scribble, maybe buried in that long reminiscence. Regardless of what stimulus produced them, these possible subjects are *you*, bits and pieces of *your* imagination, and they are *there*, waiting for you to muster the faith to take them on.

Thematic Tension

Poetry is the clear expression of mixed feelings.

W. H. Auden

There is one principle of powerful writing that should influence both your choice of subject and the way you begin to develop it. A student will sometimes ask why no one ever writes about a good time at the beach, or the happy family he or she grew up in, or the cuteness of puppies. The answer is that those subjects won't hold interest in and of themselves. When thoughts, emotions, and events flow smoothly, predictably, and, yes, pleasantly, readers get lulled by the sameness into apathy. Energy dissipates. Some unexpected force has to come along to resist or break the flow, to disturb the pattern, to introduce what we might call *thematic tension.*

In fact, wholly positive writing will not induce what the Romantic poet Samuel Taylor Coleridge called the "suspension of disbelief." He declared that the artist must create a world so vivid and full that it seems real to readers, and not just "shadows of imagination." But when the created world includes only perfect times, perfect people, and perfect pets, discriminating readers get restless, skeptical. They begin asking questions such as What about the burned-out bum on the boardwalk who accosted you three times a day? What about your brother's disaffection and your own compulsive need to achieve? What about the chewed-up boot and the stains on the rug? And intelligent readers will be left just as cold by a created world in which only the sordid, cruel, and hopeless prevail, unchallenged by the wholesome and good.

The energy in a piece of writing springs directly from the thematic tension at its heart—the tension of opposite forces pulling against each other—which may be resolved in the end or may be left in a tenuous, quivering balance. Memorable writing focuses on struggle, conflict; it is willing to confront controversy and embrace contradiction.

As we begin to make tentative decisions about a piece of writing, then, we look first for the promising signs of this deeper tension—it appears when values or ideologies clash, when one person's needs deny another's, when minds can't be made up, when difficult choices must be made. Passionate feelings and peak experiences may stimulate colorful, fluent writing, but unless they are set against other, different, even opposite, feelings and experiences, they soon lead us into pleasant dead ends.

EXERCISE: Picking Up Undercurrents

Imagine or remember an exceptionally happy time you enjoyed with friends and/or family in a specific setting, and make a list of its various moments and images, tapping all the resources you developed in Chapter 3: Coming to Our Senses to convey its positive appeal. (Your notebook may already contain the basis for such a list; you need only to play up the pleasurable images.)

Once you have captured all the positive aspects of the experience, make a list of the negative: What little things went wrong? Who was blamed? How were the problems dealt with or set right? Who worried? Was one person not having as good a time as the rest? Why not? You might even extend your list by imagining what sorts of things *might have* gone wrong. Be as specific as possible.

Try to recall a moment at which the whole experience came close to falling apart (or might have). Why did it? Why didn't it? Now draft a scene that captures what happened in the time surrounding this moment. Don't bother with elaborate exposition to introduce the scene, but see how much of the necessary information your description of characters and setting and your dialogue can reveal. As you share these writings with your group, keep track of the various ways you have embodied the nega-tive forces—accident, deprivation, human inertia, physical limitations, interpersonal conflict.

• • •

The point of this chapter is not to encourage you to be morbid or cynical, or to undercut a vision of a happy experience. The writer must rather try to infuse it with complex inner life. Remember the time you left campus one Friday with a couple of friends for a weekend of funny, bizarre adventures? Can the external adventures themselves ever be funny enough, bizarre enough, to carry an extended piece of writing? But what about the uneasiness that always hovers around a threesome: the cutting remarks that Brett kept making about your driving, and the soda Todd spilled on your backseat with hardly an apology? Did you find yourself working warily to keep the peace between the two of them, or did you feel as if they were somehow uniting against you? Who needed what from whom?

It is the tension in a experience, the fact that the pleasure or fun is won against certain odds, that it occurs *despite* certain problems, that makes it special. If pleasant times were so easy and frequent, we would take them for granted and forget them from one day to the next. Simi-larly, if pain and suffering were absolute and relentless, we would never muster the energy or desire to create. In the case of either extreme, creative writing could not exist.

Characters in Conflict

Tension is probably most readily discerned when it is embodied in *conflicts* between and within people. In his quintessential short story, "The Use of Force," William Carlos Williams focuses on the unusual "relation-ship" that springs up between a physician on a house call and a young girl with diptheria as her anxious parents hover and interfere. Stubborn with fear, the child refuses to open her mouth for examination; equally stubborn, the doctor finally resorts to force that devolves into violence, while the parents plead and apologize. The story explodes with conflict—between vulnerable child and "care-giving" adults, between her primal survival instinct and the doctor's professional pride, between her parents' ignorance and the doctor's experience.

Although these external conflicts are the most visible, other, more subtle, tensions complicate Williams's story. As its narrator, the doctor himself is torn between his need, in retrospect, to justify his actions and his need to confess. While he can take credit for saving the child's life, he is ashamed of the uncontrollable rage that her resistance provoked in him.

External and internal conflicts need not be dramatic in order to charge a poem, a story, or an essay with sufficient tension. In fact, in a notebook entry, conflicts may hover as mere hints, shadows around the edges of a description, a meditation, or an anecdote. In the following piece of freewriting by student Roberta Kleinkopf, plenty of tension hums just beneath the pleasant, nostalgic surface.

> When Father bought our first Model T Ford, the dealer had to come out every day for three days to teach him to drive it. Then Mother made Father turn around and teach her. We were one of the first to have a car in our neighborhood, and that pleased Mother immensely. She never wanted it driven in the rain or snow because the only roads were dirt, and thus muddy. But they got so dusty in summer that it wasn't much better. She was always out washing and polishing the car. The spark and gas levers were on the steering column and had to be adjusted just so before cranking. Father teased Mother about having to do all those chores for herself if she wanted to drive. She was so short that she could hardly reach the three pedals, so she sat right on the edge of the seat and hung on to the steering wheel as if she thought it was going to get away from her. Once we went to the Swan Creek picnic and there were several cars there. For a joke one of the boys stole all the keys. Mother happened to have a shoe button hook in her purse, and she persuaded Father to try inserting it into the coil box under the dash. It worked, the car started up with a cough, and we all got home that night.

Where are the subtle signs of conflict between Father and Mother? How might this writer bring that conflict into the spotlight, making it the central subject? What general references to events might be developed more fully in scenes including description of setting and dialogue? If the passage were recomposed from Father's point of view, it might elaborate the internal conflict in Father as he must choose between giving way once more to Mother's assertiveness or seeking some other way of getting home from the picnic.

Buried in this freewriting is an opportunity to resolve the conflict at least literarily: the quick summary of the picnic clamors to become a dramatic scene. The key word is *Once*, often a sign that it is time to sharpen the focus, slow the pace. Opened up with rich sensory details—setting, foods, clothing, one or two of the town's more colorful characters—as well as with closer attention to the interaction of Mother and Father, the incident at Swan Creek could become the climax of a story, an essay, or a narrative poem. Notice too that the author of this passage may realize that this incident has climactic possibilities yet begin to draft the scene without knowing exactly what form the climax will take—who will "win," who will have the last word, and what that last word will be. In fact, she will be writing in order to find out these things, with the faith that if she stays true to her characters and their circumstances, the ending will be "right."

When we can conceive our subject matter to be relationships— between characters, needs, values, behaviors—we almost guarantee dynamic writing. In Annie Dillard's essay "On a Hill Far Away," the vitality of the writing stems from the low-level but constant tension that pervades every detail of the incident it reports, an encounter between the adult author, out for a solitary walk, and a peculiar, less-than-endearing young boy. Although she would like to cut the child short and move on, his desperate attempts to engage in conversation hold her there. At the same time, the harder he tries to interest her, the more she realizes he will always be strange and lonely. Thus Dillard sets in motion a whole field of tensions—the adult's need pulling against the child's; the strain in the adult between compassion and indifference; the shuttling in the child between bravado and plea. Finally, it is this interplay of subtle forces that distinguishes the essay, not the simple affirmation it culminates with: "I thanked God for the sisters and friends I had when I was little."

EXERCISE: Reopening an Issue

Notebooks often contain cryptic references to minor revelations or resolutions: "it occurs to me that . . ." or "I wish I had known that . . ." or "from now on, I will . . ." In other words, something has happened to produce a new insight; perhaps you have changed your mind. Behind these revelations and changes of mind (or heart) lies tension—conflicts, difficult choices—that the statements have summarily resolved.

Look through your notebook for evidence of such resolutions. If nothing appropriate seems to turn up, make a list of five things you have recently realized or changed your mind about, choose one, and state it as a general principle. For example: "I didn't appreciate my family until I was away from home"; "competitive sports are no fun"; "raising a child is a thankless job"; "raising a child is the ultimate fulfillment"; "I'm going to keep quiet about things I can't change." These are not unique conclusions; countless others have come to them. What *is* unique and potentially interesting is your particular path there, starting as you did from a quite different, perhaps opposite, viewpoint.

Think of one of your own revelations or resolutions as the germ of a story, an essay, or a poem. Try writing about the struggle with yourself and/or others that led up to it, dividing the experience into three or four stages and imagining one brief but vivid scene or vignette to capture your behavior at each stage. Then compose the scene that made you, or might have made you, change your mind. Notice that in real life, big changes don't always occur as the results of "big" events. Rather they tend to build gradually, sometimes imperceptibly. And because much of our decision making takes place on an unconscious level, the actual moment of conversion may occur without any drama at all—it's only when you recall the way you spoke or acted a few months ago that you might realize you've become a different person today.

Thus in writing, you may have to combine a number of different real-life experiences in order to create your vivid scenes and their climax. You may find yourself stretching and inventing material in your preliminary stages in order to build a clear progression toward change. Take your time setting up the scene of transformation; try for the sensory concreteness of your writings in Chapter 3: Coming to Our Senses. Let the scene end *without* any explicit reference to the general insight it led you to.

Negative Capability

Even though conflicts with other people probably contribute to the final revelation in the preceding exercise, the important movement is internal as new experiences and ideas displace old. In the lyric poem and the reflective essay, the internal tension of the speaker may become the sole focus. Other characters may disappear entirely, along with definite action and thus a clear if temporary resolution.

Lewis Thomas records a rich interplay of fact, idea, and emotional response in his essay "Death in the Open," a meditation on habits of dying in the animal kingdom and habits of reacting to death. Assembling the examples of single cells, insects, birds, squirrels, elephants, and human beings, he focuses the tension inherent in his subject on the discrepancy between the relentless, astronomical amount of dying going on and its hiddenness. Fifty million human beings die every year—an "immense mass of flesh and bone and consciousness will disappear by absorption into the earth"—along with vast, inconceivable numbers of other creatures, and yet death remains an abstraction. Thomas would like to conclude:

> We will have to give up the notion that death is catastrophe, or detestable, or avoidable, or even strange. . . . There might be some comfort in the recognition of synchrony, in the information that we all go down together, in the best of company.

But he's not so sure. His meditation creates an awesome, haunting vision of death and decay as the underside of "the new life that dazzles us each morning, each spring." The animal behavior he cites implies that denial of death is as natural as death itself. Death is constant, and we cannot live with death constantly in our minds. And none of us wants to go down, no matter how fine the company. The tensions in Thomas's essay are far more complex than his stated thesis would suggest.

In conjuring more than he can logically resolve, Thomas can hardly be said to fail as a writer. Rather he is verging on the state of mind that the Romantic poet John Keats described as "negative capability": the capacity to be "in uncertainties, mysteries and doubts, without any irritable reaching after fact and reason." In other words, strong writing often records our human tendency to "be of two minds," to harbor "mixed feelings," to experience "mood swings," to wish in the face of reality. A creative writer may look so intensely and long at an object or situation, pay such attention to all associated images, all possibilities for meaning and judgment, that previous assumptions about it dissolve and he or she is left with a sense of paradox.

Read closely the following poem by James Wright, a carefully detailed record of the particular moment announced in the title.

Lying in a Hammock at William Duffy's Farm in Pine Island, Minnesota

Over my head, I see the bronze butterfly,
Asleep on the black trunk,
Blowing like a leaf in green shadow.
Down the ravine behind the empty house,

The cowbells follow one another
Into the distances of the afternoon.
To my right,
In a field of sunlight between two pines,
The droppings of last year's horses
Blaze up into golden stones.
I lean back, as the evening darkens and comes on.
A chicken hawk floats over, looking for home.
I have wasted my life.

Note the complex sensory appeal of these images, their colors, sounds, texture, temperature, and even smell. Yet they are more than the details of a rural retreat. There is something not quite pleasant about them, not quite what we expect. "Bronze" is quietly fighting with "butterfly" and "flowing," not to mention its clash with "black" and "green." Through which other images does Wright sustain this moment's tension? His opening lines mix stillness and motion, organic and inorganic, light and dark. What other opposites are held in balance in this poem? How does this continuous tension reflect on what the speaker is "telling" us in the last line? Though it sounds like a classic thesis statement, ambivalence riddles the images that lead up to it, and we wonder: Has he wasted his life by lying around in hammocks? or by not lying around in hammocks enough? Can he perhaps be telling us that he is not committing himself to one possibility or the other, that he's never quite sure?

Our conscious reasoning mind, hungry for resolution, might insist on the "irritable reaching" for a single answer: *either* the speaker in Wright's poem is intensely enjoying his moment of solitude and stillness *or* he's feeling guilty about it. But the tension sustained by the images reminds us that emotional truths are not simple. Feelings are paradoxical. We must be receptive to a full range of contradictory possibilities— expanding, as Keats put it, our capacity for uncertainty—both to appreciate and to create a strong poem, story, or essay.

Discerning tension is the first stage of preparation for the zero-draft. We always write about tension on some level; it is the energy source for our created worlds. Though we often exaggerate real-life tensions as we bring them into central focus, they do not need to have apocalyptic dimensions to power an essay, a story, or a poem. The conflicts, choices, and changes need not lead to divorce, murder, or treason. What central tension will do is foster purposeful movement, whether external action or internal reflection, and suggest some sort of resolution. It gets us started with some reassurance that we will discover a rich middle, and even if temporary and provisional, an end.

NOTEBOOK OPTIONS

1. Try the opposite of the first exercise in this chapter: begin with a vivid rendition of a horrible experience, and play up all its disastrous, painful elements. Then make a list of everything positive you can think of about the experience (a well-meaning character, fine weather, a moment of hope), inventing if you wish, trying different points of view. Weave these positive images into your original writing, letting them pull against the currents of disaster.
2. Make a list of five tough choices you have faced in the last year. Select one, and write about the "road not taken." Make a list tabulating the imaginary chain of consequences that might have followed if you had chosen the other alternative. Draft a detailed portrait, in the third person, of the self you would be right now had you followed the alternative path. Include setting and action.
3. The memorable characters in literature are those that provoke mixed feelings in readers—love and hate, support and disapproval. These are characters whose creators, possessed of Keats's "negative capability," refrained from forcing them to be good or bad, strong or weak, serious or playful, but instead instilled them with the complex life of all of the above. Bring to mind or imagine a character you admire. Make a list of his or her admirable actions, wonderful one-time things this person has done as well as things he or she does regularly. Then make a list of his or her actions that you don't admire; you may have to make yourself exaggerate what you consider little, insignificant foibles. Freewrite about this person, letting yourself slip back and forth between positive and negative, developing material from each list as the impulse moves you.
4. Now try the reverse of option 3: begin with a person you dislike or disdain, then balance the portrait with positive material.
5. Keep a list of issues you can't make up your mind about—whether to quit your job, stop eating meat, tell someone off, major in English, try psychotherapy, admit a parent into a nursing home. Choose one issue, and create a verbal picture for each alternative: what you see, hear, smell, taste, and feel happening if you commit yourself to one alternative; then to the other. These pictures do not need to be realistic; let your imagination offer its details.

Chapter 7

Showing versus Telling

The calculated coercion of the senses is the fundamental technique of all art.

Jacques Barzun, *The Use and Abuse of Art*

Writing is seduction: it invites the reader to suspend disbelief, to surrender to an illusion, to be tricked into imagining that a mother and daughter really are arguing bitterly, or a man in a shabby tuxedo really is playing "Eleanor Rigby" on a harmonica, or a lion really is stalking a zebra—when all the while this reader is merely processing words on a page.

Writing in Pictures

Be literalists of the imagination.

Marianne Moore

In this chapter, we return to our senses with a new emphasis. Our senses not only lead us out of ourselves, as we saw in Chapter 3: Coming to Our Senses, to discover the variety and richness in the world around us; they also give substance to the particular, personal worlds that each of us tries to create in words. Through sensory images, writers share their "alternative" worlds with their readers. In other words, once we have learned to activate our own senses, we need to consider the ways we can activate our readers' senses to transform the abstract hieroglyphics we type onto a page into irresistibly "real" experiences. As we begin to think and feel and write in concrete terms—from simple images to full-blown scenes—we draw our readers into a gut-level involvement with our created world; our words take on flesh. Concrete details become the fertile

65

soil for what the American poet Marianne Moore called "imaginary gardens with real toads in them."

Respect for concrete detail, interestingly enough, translates into respect for our readers. We refrain from forcing a grand "universal" theme on our readers, offering them instead the sensory data, the simulated experience, from which to derive that theme. In other words, we don't *tell* our readers what to think or feel; we *show* them concretely an image, an action, even a gesture, as precisely as we see it, and trust that they will be led to draw if not the same conclusions we do, at least meaningful ones. We create a compelling alternative world, then invite our readers to judge and interpret it.

The word *compelling* deserves extra emphasis: respect for readers, a willingness to allow them to make up their own minds, is *not* a license to be *vague*. Quite the contrary. Try to be clear and precise about the worlds you create in words. The title of James Wright's poem in the preceding chapter, "Lying in a Hammock at William Duffy's Farm in Pine Island, Minnesota," anticipates the pains the poet will take to render the concrete details of that evening in full detail. The objective of Lewis Thomas's essay "Death in the Open" is to assault our tendency to keep death a vague abstraction; to do this he conjures a Noah's Ark of mortal animals, as well as assorted mind-bending statistics.

If we write to introduce our readers to the world as we perceive it, why leave it blurry? Though we must allow our readers to decide what our poems, stories, and essays finally mean, we don't make them guess about basic facts. In "Gryphon," a story drawn from childhood about a bizarre substitute teacher, Charles Baxter establishes the story's time with revealing exactitude:

> On Wednesday afternoon, between the geography lesson on ancient Egypt's hand-operated irrigation system and an art project that involved drawing a model city next to a mountain, our fourth-grade teacher, Mr. Hibler, developed a cough.

Mary Robison brings place into equally sharp focus in her story "Happy Boy, Allen," in which an alienated young man tries to make emotional contact with his alcoholic aunt:

> Mindy was propped on her couch, on foam pillows the colors of Easter candy. She had a crocheted afghan spun twice around the calves of her legs. The old suite she rented had been restyled with lowered ceilings and a pink-beige carpet. There was a new folding door on the bathroom, and a line of little appliances in the kitchen.

In Annie Dillard's essay "On a Hill Far Away," mentioned in the preceding chapter, the facts of time and place are crucial: the bleakness of the rural landscape in January, the barbed wire fence that separates her from the lonely boy, the darkening day that gives her the excuse to leave him, even though "the creek below held a frail color still, the memory of a light that hadn't yet been snuffed." As each of these excerpts shows, details of setting not only offer our readers clear, vivid pictures, they establish time, create atmosphere, convey impressions, and suggest ideas. In Baxter's story, they ask us to recall the earnest irrelevance of grade school; in Robison's, they point up tawdriness and pretense. In Dillard's essay, they enforce the hopelessness of the child's isolation. In each, the sensory experience begins to expand into an emotional one.

EXERCISE: Embodying Abstractions

Reread several pages of your notebook, and make a list of any abstractions you find, words that stand for general ideas, like *caution, disapproval, indecision, love, order, passion, pollution, resilience, sadness,* and *serenity.* Notice that these are the tidy, bloodless conclusions that you have drawn about certain experiences. Select several, and try to retrieve some of the messy vitality each has for you. Make a list of the concrete images or examples that each brings to mind, forgetting about logic. For example, for you *purity* might mean a turquoise lake in upper Wisconsin, the smell of alcohol, a flawless quartz, your first romantic relationship, a crazed racist, a perfectly executed football play, clean sheets, or perhaps gold. Read your lists aloud, and enjoy their energy and complexity, both of which are sadly lost when you resort to abstractions.

• • •

The following is a draft of a poem in which a student writer explores the concept of freedom—the way freedom means different things to different people; the way the expression of individual freedom can lead to conflict; the way individual freedom is restrained by law. He never mentions these issues, however; instead he offers us the behavior of some of the colorful inhabitants of his own hometown. We get the picture.

> Walter Keller from Hell's Corner plants
> it with his tobacco though he still grumbles
> about fertilizer taxes and the new bag limit on whitetail.
> Pervis savors it at the South Boston Speedway
> as he sits holding a bologna burger with his feet

propped on a cooler of Milwaukee's Best.
It all tastes the same.

But he chose
it like John Brown did that rambling old
shack on Mecklenburg Avenue where he sells his shoes.
Actually, back
when school buses and water fountains
were color coded Mr. Brown didn't have it but
now he drives it in his Jaguar,
the only one in town.

That's freedom for you. Today
he chuckles at backwards folks
like Roland Chester whose colors
have not yet run.

Old Roland took the liberty
of running over John Brown's neighbor last
week and now walks to Wright's Superette
instead of cruising oblivious
at 20 miles an hour, arm waving
and voice bellowing like a deer
hound.

His truck with the gun rack rusts in the drive
and Roland waits on his porch for hunting season
and that preserve where he'll shoot 20 mourning doves.
There's a little of it left in swinging on his porch
and throwing curses in his worn tank T-shirt at the lean,
    mean
Jaguar as it passes and kicks up
gravel on his lawn. But just
a little because he chooses no change.

                                             James Wellons

Developing Summary

Showing means writing in pictures instead of abstractions; it also
means slowing down and taking a second, deeper, and more detailed look
at experiences we have taken for granted. We may find ourselves search-
ing desperately through our notebooks for something novel to write
about, when it is right there on the page we just turned past, dismissed by

summary. Imagine, for example, the rich comic possibilities in opening up the following summary of habitual action, capped by a judgmental abstraction: "I used to hate it when everyone in my family sat down to dinner together. No one bothered with manners; everyone talked at once. It was mass confusion." Shown rather than told, the first two sentences might become the basis for a whole story in which characters are named and described, their bad manners are specifically portrayed, and the dialogue crackles with crazy *non sequiturs.* To make the scene even more concrete and immediate, it might be composed in the present tense.

Notice how a summary sentence like "I was furious that she'd read my mail, and I told her so" might become more compelling if expanded before the reader's senses as a brief scene in the present tense:

> Slowly she produces the opened letter from her bathrobe pocket, her head tipped slightly back so she can look down at me the whole time with a cold gray stare. She smells faintly of menthol. I snatch the folded sheet from her hand and glare back.
>
> "What, did they cancel your soaps?" I ask. "Didn't you have anything better to do today than read my mail?"

EXERCISE: Opening Up Summary

Return to a piece of writing you like from Chapter 4: Remembering, and check every sentence not only for traces of abstraction and generalization but also for summarized action—in other words, telling that stands in for more vivid, dramatic showing. Telltale signs of summary are references to habitual action like *each morning* or *every weekend* and verbs accompanied by the auxiliary *would.* ("Each morning he would help her get dressed.") When you find such a reference, *open it up* to whatever details, gestures, and scenes come to mind, and record them in the simple past or present tense. ("That morning, he squeezed an exact worm of toothpaste onto her brush for her. Then he counted out a bright assortment of her pills.") Instead of describing *all* Saturdays, commit yourself to a specific, if an imaginary, composite one. Notice that when you shift from telling to showing, words sprout into sentences, sentences branch into paragraphs, paragraphs ripen into scenes.

• • •

When we allow chosen moments to unfold their endless possibilities, we give up a certain conscious control, because so many of these possibilities are unforeseeable. Memories may retrieve things we have lived a long time forgetting; imagination may fill in gaps in puzzling ways.

One character gets defensive and tries to leave, another rolls up his sleeves and reveals a strange tattoo. An old man appears who acts like your grandfather. Maybe hailstones shower down; maybe a panther slouches across a golf course. "I know just what I'm going to write about," a student claims, envisioning a wild, dangerously generic spree. And he is off to a fast start, with a first paragraph that ends, "He stopped at a crossroads town to grab some lunch and fill up with gas and then sped on, his thoughts on Mexico."

But what was the town called, what did its structures look like, what was its weather, and how did it smell? How many human beings did he see, and what were they like? Were there any animals? Who served him lunch, how did it taste, whom did he speak to, and what did they say? Did anyone ask him where he was going and why? Did anyone give him trouble? How did he get out of it? What happens to this writer's intentions if he decides to develop this scene instead of glossing over it in favor of what he knows? He may find out some subtle and surprising things about his main character; his main character may not even have to cross the border in order to be challenged and changed.

Truly original discoveries often come when we go against the grain of preconceptions, when we slow down our pace and explore the details of character and place, the back-and-forth of dialogue. Like grass coming up through the cracks in the cement squares of a sidewalk, the quirky, powerful life in a piece of writing may be trying to push through where we never expected it, where we didn't even want it, because we preferred the efficiency of control.

It may take some practice to get used to an experimental "literalism" of the imagination. Some new writers resist it. They think of the great literary artists and their lofty and universal themes, they think of love and death and the purpose of life, and they are sure they want to begin way up there, writing about important things. Concrete pictures, specific examples, feel like a comedown, childish simplifications, or else needless filler. Such writers are primed for frustration: they may come up with a few sentences that capture the essence of their chosen theme, then be stymied as to how to develop them. More often than not, they sit and stare at a blank page.

Too much cosmic truth can be fatal to the writer. William Butler Yeats transformed this abstract principle into concrete drama in a poem called "A Dialogue of Self and Soul." The earthy self is fascinated by the things of this world:

> The consecrated blade upon my knees
> Is Sato's ancient blade, still as it was,

Still razor-keen, still like a looking-glass
Unspotted by the centuries;
That flowering, silken, old embroidery, torn
From some court-lady's dress and round
The wooden scabbard bound and wound,
Can, tattered, still protect, faded adorn.

The mystical soul, on the other hand, who can appreciate only the abstract meanings of things, is determined to rise above the everyday life of the senses, "the crime of death and birth." Yet when the soul manages, halfway through the poem, to ascend to heaven, his "tongue's a stone."

Maybe this mystic philosopher is silenced because a perfect heaven undoes the tension that activates writing. Maybe he is silenced because for the disembodied soul in the disembodied world of heaven, there is nothing to write about. In both cases, Yeats hints at the frustration in tackling abstract ideas head-on in poetry.

When Telling Works

If concrete growing has the power to spark life in our writing, it also has its limits. There are times when showing has already served to uncover productive tension, and to open an image or scene to further detail will simply introduce competing tension and confusion. Consider again the student whose narrative has stopped to look around a border town on its way to Mexico. Suppose he observes two men arguing in the lunchroom and can hear every accusation of betrayal, every reference to past failure. But also suppose his narrative has already found its focus in the ten-year-old boy who has followed him in and sat down opposite him and asked him, "Are you Superman?" Then the narrator might be allowed to say, "In the corner two men kept pounding their table with their fists," and be done with it. If their argument cannot be made to reflect in some way on the narrator's response to the boy, they must be relegated to filling in the background.

There are also instances when further detail doesn't necessarily confuse, but simply bogs writing down. Experienced writers know intuitively when to surrender conscious control in order to see what turns up and when to take control confidently in order to move the writing along, making the most of generalizations like "it was a snowy day in midwinter" or "the room was stiff and tidy as a sitcom set," summary transitions like "three winters later" or "after dinner had been cleared away and everyone but Tom and Jerry had staked out a place to sleep for the night," or simply the white space between stanzas in a poem. Perhaps nothing relevant to the poem's subject occurred in those three years, and though cleaning up a kitchen after a meal could be the source of some richly disgusting imagery, the conflict between Tom and Jerry might not have revealed itself in the process.

Experienced writers sense when it is appropriate to step back from the created world, in all its sensory detail, and offer comments about it. In fact, this shift in perspective is the main strategy of the traditional essay, which develops a general thesis statement by embodying it in various concrete ways. It is also the basis for the traditional expository paragraph—general assertion as topic sentence plus specific examples. In a persuasive essay, this alternation may be the perfect means to increase clarity and force, a sort of one-two punch. In less coercive writing, however, assertive telling in addition to concrete showing may have the weakening effect of redundance.

Lacking experience with this alternation of showing and telling, new writers rely on feedback from a writers' group or writing class to "keep them honest," to inform them when they are skipping over the difficult but necessary details, when the bare bones of their writing need a little flesh. But how do new writers know a scene is *not* necessary, when the details included are sufficient to induce belief and concern, and, in fact, any further detail will be dead weight?

When Showing Works

It is not merely a materialistic handling of objects that is the base for writing, but using details to step through to the other shore.
Natalie Goldberg, *Writing Down the Bones*

Though the response of a trusted reader is invaluable in selecting details, there is one principle writers can apply themselves—a variation on William Carlos Williams's prescription for concreteness, "No idea, but in things." In urging his fellow poets to avoid ponderous abstract telling in favor of showing by means of clear and precise sensory images, Williams was also hinting at a reverse rule of thumb: No things unless ideas are in them.

In the following poem by Ted Kooser, the contrast between telling and showing becomes the subject itself, as the speaker translates for his audience the messages implicit in the small world he surveys:

Abandoned Farmhouse

He was a big man, says the size of his shoes
on a pile of broken dishes by the house;
a tall man too, says the length of the bed
in an upstairs room; and a good, God-fearing man,
says the Bible with a broken back
on the floor below the window, dusty with sun;
but not a man for farming, say the fields
cluttered with boulders and the leaky barn.

A woman lived with him, says the bedroom wall
papered with lilacs and the kitchen shelves
covered with oilcloth, and they had a child,
says the sandbox made from a tractor tire.
Money was scarce, say the jars of plum preserves
and canned tomatoes sealed in the cellar-hole,
and the winters cold, say the rags in the window frames.
It was lonely here, says the narrow gravel road.

Something went wrong, says the empty house
in the weed-choked yard. Stones in the fields
say he was not a farmer; the still-sealed jars
in the cellar say she left in a nervous heat.
And the child? Its toys are strewn in the yard
like branches after a storm—a rubber cow,
a rusty tractor with a broken plow,
a doll in overalls. Something went wrong, they say.

As writers, then, we can almost assume that all things mean; showing will tell what they mean. Perhaps part of our reverence for the concrete stems from the conviction expressed by William Blake, that we can "see the world in a Grain of Sand, and a heaven in a Wild Flower." We all indulge in these magical equations on some level. We fill time capsules with various documents and artifacts and place them in cornerstones or launch them into space. By the same selection process, sensory details are retained by a final, "polished" piece of writing. They are there not only for liveliness and credibility but also because they radiate significance.

The following poem by Gary Snyder consists of three vivid sensory images:

A ringing tire iron
        dropped on the pavement

> Whang of a saw
> brusht on limbs
>
>> the taste
>> of rust.

What do these images mean? Do they suggest a single abstract theme? What title might you give this poem? What are the strengths of Snyder's title: "Some Good Things to Be Said for the Iron Age"?

EXERCISE: From Summary to Scene

Make a list of twenty-five concrete nouns, aiming for diversity. If you wish, you can turn back to material from Chapter 3: Coming to Our Senses to enrich your assortment. Beside each "thing," write the first three or four "ideas" that come to mind. Don't worry about logic. For example, *parking meter* may provoke the thoughts *hassle, law and order, paranoia, accidents*. Choose one of these nouns that seems promising to you, visualize it specifically, and arrange objects or people around it in a concrete scene, reaching for those specific details that will reinforce your general ideas.

Does it make any difference, for example, if the parking meter is silver, if the time on it has expired, if it is out of order, if the pole is bent and rusted, if the meter itself has actually been ripped off the pole, if a Cadillac is parked there or an old Chevy missing a tire or your car with a boot locked on its rear wheel, if someone has dropped a quarter on the pavement, if you hear a siren in the background, or if there is so much gritty, unplowed snow in the space that no one can park there? (Remember that details can register on all five of the senses.) Take turns reading these descriptions and entertaining suggestions from your group as to what ideas they embody, what they might mean.

•   •   •

Creative writers develop the habit of thinking concretely, in images rather than abstract ideas. They show their readers an imaginative facsimile of the world instead of telling them about the world, and this choice, paradoxically, makes their writing both more subtle and more potent, less coercive yet irresistible. For as Chapter 5: Dreaming Awake reminds us, images are our primal language; they appeal to a reader on a gut-emotional level. And choosing to show instead of tell does not require giving up on abstract meaning. Far from it. Every *thing* means. It is the coincidence of vivid concreteness and meaning that gives those black-and-white marks on a page the power to cause chills, the quickening pulse, laughter, and tears.

NOTEBOOK OPTIONS

1. When learning to render a likeness, the student artist spends hours in the studio training to be attentive to every gesture: the relation of one finger to the next, the precise tilt of the head. Begin a collection of postures and/or gestures that indicate or suggest a person's particular emotional state. In other words, how does a person look or act when feeling afraid, angry, sad, joyous, frustrated, content, curious, stubborn, reckless? You may want to include "props" in your descriptions.
2. Think about the routines you regularly engage in—brushing your teeth, fixing breakfast, feeding your pets, executing a specific task at work. Do you have a special way of performing one of these routines? Make a list of the steps you take, breaking the process down into its smallest details, emphasizing those that represent a departure from the "normal" or obvious way of performing it. As you *show* these quirky habits, do they *tell* anything about you? Imagine someone different from you performing this routine. What would she or he do differently?
3. Make a list to corroborate the following sentence: "Character X expressed contempt for authority in a number of little ways." Or try the opposite: "Character X liked to express respect for authority in a number of little ways."
4. Imagine that you are a private detective investigating a person by snooping around the rooms that person regularly inhabits. The person might be yourself, someone you know well, or a fictional composite. Make a lengthy list of the items you find; study your list for a while in order to let the full picture sink into your imagination; then select about ten items that seem particularly revealing, and see what you can deduce from them. Try to go beyond the obvious equations such as "lots of books, therefore likes to read." Does the evidence point to a possible crime, or as in the poem "The Abandoned Farmhouse," to something going wrong? Allow yourself to put two and two together and get five, to make imaginative, comical, or bizarre leaps. Remember to check drawers and closets.
5. Showing instead of telling is the strategy of dreams. As we sleep, our imaginations regale us with strange sequences and combinations of images, all of which can be interpreted to reveal things about our real-life situations, past, present, and/or future. Turn inward, and concentrate on your emotional state at this moment, jotting down what

balance you find of happy, sad, angry, powerful, frustrated, and hurt feelings. Try to invent a dream that represents concretely the pieces of your emotional puzzle and the way they all fit together. You needn't confine yourself to images drawn from your real-life situation. Remember that except for concreteness, dreams may suspend all rules of plausible narrative.

6. Select several of the most vivid, expressive examples from your list of related images from the first exercise in this chapter. Arrange them in a brief concrete poem along the lines of Gary Snyder's formula for the Iron Age, complete with an appropriate, "telling" title.

Chapter 8

Making Connections

*A completely unique object, if such a thing were imaginable,
could not be described. Lacking metaphoric connections, it would
remain inexpressible.*

N. Katherine Hayles, *Chaos Bound*

The earliest lessons we learned as children taught us (often through picture books and always through the medium of words) to differentiate cats from dogs, zebras from giraffes, boys from girls, safe from dangerous, good from bad, life from death. In school, we learned to separate "language arts" and numbers, work and recess, smart and dumb. Later, we distinguished Jewish from Moslem from Christian, communism from democracy. Now we are invited to divide our "true" selves from our practical jobs, and our lives into the tidy upward steps on a career ladder.

Despite all this compartmentalization, we still experience moments of unity and vision when, as the Victorian poet and essayist Matthew Arnold might say, we see life steadily and see it whole. We erase from our minds the boundaries we have learned to draw around ourselves and others, things organic and inorganic, and try for a moment to perceive their interconnectedness. We may find this moment alone in a natural setting, or in a group of people with whom we compose an audience, congregation, or parade.

Such moments inspire us to write, to try to induce in a reader something akin to our own mystical perception, by embodying it in sensory images and/or scenes. In the following poem, "The Family Is All There Is," Pattiann Rogers gives visible and palpable shape to such an apprehension of unity:

Think of those old, enduring connections
found in all flesh—the channeling
wires and threads, vacuoles, granules,
plasma and pods, purple veins, ascending
boles and coral sapwood (sugar-
and light-filled), those common ligaments,
filaments, fibers and canals.

Seminal to all kin also is the open
mouth—in heart urchin and octopus belly,
in catfish, moonfish, forest lily,
and rugosa rose, in thirsty magpie,
wailing cat cub, barker, yodeler
yawning coati.

And there is a pervasive
clasping common to the clan—the heart nails
of lichen and ivy sucker
on the church wall, the bean tendril
and the taproot, the bolted coupling
of crane files, the hold of the shearwater
on its morning squid, guanine
to cytosine, adenine to thymine,
fingers around fingers, the grip of
the voice on presence, the grasp
of the self on place.

Remember the same hair on pygmy
dormouse and yellow-necked caterpillar,
covering red baboon, thistle seed
and willow herb? Remember the similar
snorts of warthog, walrus, male moose
and sumo wrestler? Remember the familiar
whinny and shimmer found in river birches,
bay mares and bullfrog tadpoles,
in children playing at shoulder tag
on a summer lawn?

The family—weavers, reachers, winders
and connivers, pumpers, runners, air
and bubble riders, rock-sitters, wave-gliders,
wire-wobblers, soothers, flagellators—all
brothers, sisters, all there is.

Name something else.

The Metaphorical Habit of Mind

Plenty of poems, stories, and essays are not about transcending our divided everyday lives; they are about managing within their restrictions, bogged in what William Butler Yeats called "complexities of mire and blood." In other words, most writing does not try to encompass the world, but rather concentrates on one particular fragment. Yet even when our subject is not visionary, our literary practice is. In other words, Rogers's poem is not only the expression of a glorious epiphany; it is also a treasury of similarities waiting to be discovered by the writer: the forest lily might open like a catfish mouth; the yodeler might wail like a cat cub; fingers might wind around someone's arm like bean tendrils; the wind through the birches might sound like whinnying horses.

This chapter explores the way creative writing channels the sense of wholeness into a set of powerful literary techniques. Through metaphor, simile, personification, and analogy, creative writing reconnects the fragments, discovering, building, and even forcing bonds among disparate things, people, and events. Just as the preceding chapter urged a concrete habit of mind, then, this chapter celebrates the *metaphorical* one. The ability to see original and ingenious connections between things adds clarity, liveliness, tension, and depth to our treatment of material. It may also lead to new insight, material we never thought we had in us. No idea, but in the juxtapositions of things.

In the poem "Indian Summer at Land's End" by Stanley Kunitz, notice the connections Kunitz makes to capture the particular texture of a complex mood. How often do we respond to a change of season with melancholy and nostalgia, as if the unpredictable weather has called the present into question and set us wandering into the future and past? The general experience may be familiar, but Kunitz's metaphorical vision renews and intensifies its poignancy.

> The season stalls, unseasonably fair,
> blue-fair, serene, a stack of golden discs,
> each disc a day, and the addition slow.
> I wish you were here with me to walk the flats,
> towards dusk especially when the tide is out
> and the bay turns opal, filled with rolling fire
> that washes on the mouldering wreck offshore,
> our mussel-vineyard, strung with bearded grapes.
> Last night I reached for you and shaped you there
> lying beside me as we drifted past
> the farthest seamarks and the watchdog bells,

> and round Long Point throbbing its frosty light,
> until we streamed into the open sea.
> What did I know of voyaging till now?
> Meanwhile I tend my flock, small golden puffs
> impertinent as wrens, with snipped-off tails,
> who bounce down from the trees. High overhead,
> on the trackless roads, skywriting V and yet
> another V, the southbound Canada express
> hoots of horizons and distances. . . .

Though the mood itself may not surprise us, its connections and their evolution do, as the focus shifts from the beauty and serenity of those late summer days—solid gold coins, accumulating steadily—to their evanescence. Once the speaker has recalled the lost and longed-for "you," the days become "golden" cloud "puffs," an undifferentiated and docile flock as impertinent as wrens—irrelevant and out of line. What are distinct and relevant are the harbingers of the winter ahead, the V's of Canada geese flying south (as inexorably as trains) and hooting of unnamable "horizons and distances."

The preceding chapter suggested that shifting from telling to showing often serves to bring out interesting tensions latent in a piece of rough writing. Kunitz's poetic description of Indian summer shows how making connections cuts another path to the same goal.

Metaphor and Simile

The term *metaphor* is often used in a general sense to describe the connecting habit of mind and its results. It also denotes a specific kind of connection, the fusion of two things based on as little as a single similarity, to the extent that one is spoken of in terms of the other. Most of the connections in "Indian Summer at Land's End" are metaphors, asserting the identity of days with discs, mussels with grapes, sunlight on the water with "rolling fire," life with a water voyage, days with cloud puffs, and geese with some sort of skytrain.

A *simile,* on the other hand, is the explicit connection of two things by means of *like* or *as*—which allows Kunitz to call his waning days "impertinent as wrens, with snipped tails," bouncing down from the trees.

Similes probably think of themselves as the metaphor's older sibling, ambitious yet dutiful, clearly the firstborn of the two. Once the simile exists, after all, the *like* or *as* can be trimmed to produce the more ornery, volatile metaphor. Metaphors themselves, however, rooted as they are in our earliest mental processes, would probably argue for their own priority, claiming that similes are merely their own tamed offshoots, cultivated by the grown-up, rational mind.

In whichever form these connections arise, they grow out of the same place, the same imaginative experience. The two items they connect may be quite disparate, their similarity tenuous; as in Kunitz's poem, the fusions may initially feel like confusion—coins, grapes, birds, and express trains, all set against the vivid sensory images of Land's End. Yet beneath the diversity, the imagination has grasped unity, consistency— the reality of movement and change. To fall for an illusion of permanent summer is about as silly as hoarding money. The speaker walks the flats, the tide ebbs and flows, clouds drift, wrens bounce down, geese soar, while speaker and beloved stream into the ocean sea.

As we experiment with metaphors and similes, we discover that each figure of speech has its special power. In the following poem by Langston Hughes, first similes and then a metaphor evoke concrete images of African-American experience to embody the abstraction "a dream deferred." How does the poem highlight the different effects of these figures of speech?

Harlem

What happens to a dream deferred?

Does it dry up
like a raisin in the sun?
Or fester like a sore—
And then run?
Does it stink like rotten meat?
Or crust and sugar over—
like a syrupy sweet?

Maybe it just sags like a heavy load.

Or does it explode?

EXERCISE: Similes

The following is a list of adjectives set up to be turned into similes. Add your own ten or fifteen favorites, and then complete them (in a couple of different ways, if you wish) quickly, without worrying about whether your comparisons are original or not.

> as orange as
> as barren as
> as hungry as
> as fragile as
> as arrogant as
> as rough as
> as tentative as
> as pliant as
> as eloquent as
> as reliable as
> as restless as
> as confining as
> as pale as

Once you have a substantial list, try mixing and matching the adjectives and nouns. Do you find any interesting results? For example: "as pale as an empty playground," "as arrogant as a Boy Scout," "as restless as pantyhose?" Choose your five favorites, and share them with your classmates, discussing the implications of the tension their joining has aroused. How *do* they make sense?

Now that you have a random assortment of nouns, try mixing and matching them in the form of metaphors to produce interestingly suggestive results. Is a Boy Scout "an empty playground"? Could a sunset be "a desert" or a preacher be "asphalt"? "Poetry," said Carl Sandburg, "is the synthesis of hyacinths and biscuits." Pick one or two of your forced connections that seem to work and try extending them, describing your first object further in terms of the second.

•   •   •

Although metaphors, similes, and other figures of speech have always distinguished the language of poetry, they are not its exclusive domain. When a story or an essay shifts into the description of setting or the narration of events, its language often reaches for the extra power of metaphor. The following examples, plucked from the story "Turning Out," by Gayle Whittier, describe first a star ballet student:

the whole staff of her body blossoms, deft porcelain, ivory;

and then her instructor:

Madame, massively caryatid, emerges from the office in her magenta satin class dress, flamethrower hair, thighs muscular with varicose grapes.

The extra connections here bring a sensuous intensity that literal descrip‑
tion might never accomplish: we don't just *see* the differences between the
two women, we *feel* them, in both senses of that verb. The metaphorical
habit of mind can enliven and elaborate any subject, plumb its dimensions.

EXERCISE: Metaphors

Make a list of objects that are important to you for emotional or
symbolic reasons. They may be associated with your childhood, a person
you cherish, an activity that lifts you out of yourself, or perhaps a single
event or moment you will never forget. They might range from an automo‑
bile to the mug half-filled with coffee on the desk beside you now.

Choose one of the objects and dwell on it, turn it upside down and
get inside it, in your imagination and with your senses too, if the object is
available for actual study. Compose a series of ten to fifteen metaphors
equating your object to something else: "My running shoes are boats to
heaven and hell, skiffs without rudders; they are straightjackets for my
paranoid-schizophrenic feet; they are barnyards of microscopic compost;
they are stiffened, elaborate socks; they are designer calluses, synthetic
peat pots," and so on. Loosen the hold of practicality and logic, follow
your intuition, bring in the objects you associate with the one you have
chosen. If this one object runs dry of connections, try another. You might
try this exercise with a subject you have already begun to write about in
your notebook, as a way of opening it up in fertile directions.

EXERCISE: Character by Association

Think of a person you know well, and answer the following ques‑
tions about him or her, following your intuition rather than any rational
analysis. Focus on answering not in terms of what this person likes or
prefers, or who this person thinks he or she is, but rather in terms of *your
impression* of him or her.

If this person were an animal, which would he or she be?
If he or she were a flower?
A tree?
A color?
A food?
A country?
A body of water?
A figure from history?

Something porcelain?
An article of clothing?

Picture this person next in a real-life setting that is typical for him or her, and draft a description, weaving in some of your more interesting intuitive connections. Again, you might focus this exercise on a character you have already begun to develop in your notebook, as a way of discovering new dimensions.

Personification

Traditionally, *personification* is the figure of speech that describes the nonhuman or abstract by using human characteristics, and thus familiarly tangible terms—a device ideally designed to convert telling to showing. In the following poem, John Haines takes on the formidable abstraction "springtime"—formidable because it has been done and overdone—and creates a fresh rendition of its richness through personification.

And When the Green Man Comes

The man is clothed
in birchbark,
small birds cling to his limbs
and one builds
a nest in his ear.

The clamor of bedlam
infests his hair, a wind
blowing in his head
shakes down
a thought that turns
to moss and lichen
at his feet.

His eyes are blind
with April,
his breath distilled
of butterflies
and bees, and in his beard
the maggot sings.

He comes again
with litter of chips
and empty cans,
his shoes full of mud and dung;

an army of shedding dogs
attends him,
the valley shudders where
he stands,
redolent of roses,
exalted in
the streaming rain.

The accumulated detail of this personification captures the life, the *tension* of spring. Spring is not just pretty and romantic; it brings shedding dogs and litter. The organic renewal it promises is, quite accurately, one of "mud and dung," eased by maggots. It is no wonder the "valley shudders" to give up the frozen peace and quiet of winter.

Analogy

Metaphorical connections are often quick, explosive, their purpose to capture the essence of a subject that might never come across by more rational, discursive means. This is not to say that writers always allow their imaginations free reign or that effective connections cannot be the carefully planned collaborations between reason and the imagination. *Analogies,* or extended comparisons, appeal to the rational, practical mind as well as to the intuitive. Whereas many of the connections posited by poetic metaphor might not survive outside the unique matrix of their particular work, analogies claim more general relevance: metaphors and similes tend to enliven the known and familiar by means of unexpected, sometimes mysterious associations, whereas analogies tend to clarify the complex and esoteric by means of associations to the known and familiar.

In "The Bike," an essay by Timothy Foote, a young man resorts to a simile and a metaphor, capped by a dramatic analogy, in order to convey to his anxious and skeptical father the problematic appeal of a motorcycle.

On a bike you flow, the engine sound rising and falling like a sax, an overwhelming spring of raw power, tappable by a twist of the wrist. It is the feeling you have when holding a loaded and cocked twelve-gauge: wired tight, conscious of the potential, the delicate control over a force greater than the force of the self yet under the self's control. An electric pulse hurtles from brain to hand and the force is no longer potential. The gun booms, kicking back, the shot tearing through whatever you aim at; a quick, pained yelp as the meat on the back tire claws for a grip on the asphalt.

Assuming that his father enjoys firing a shotgun, the son designs an analogy to explain and justify his love of bikes: he describes the unknown or complex in terms of the known or simpler. This strategy is not confined to the expository purposes of the essay; a character in fiction or poetry certainly qualifies as a complex unknown, an elusive entity that an apt analogy might capture for a lucid moment. The story "Inexorable Progress," by Mary Hood, records the slow emotional deterioration of Angelina, a woman misunderstood by husband, daughter, and friends. In fact, when Angelina attempts suicide, "no one had the least notion. They called around when she failed to show up at the Tupperware party." Hood opens her story about this deceptively simple woman with a grim analogy:

> There's not much difference between a bare tree and a dead tree in winter. Only when the others begin to leaf out the next spring, and one is left behind in the general green onrush, can the eye tell. By then it is too late for remedy. That's how it was with Angelina: a tree stripped to the natural bone, soul-naked in the emptying wind. She was good at pretending: she hung color and approximations of seasonal splendor on every limb, and swayed like a bower in the autumn gales around her, but her heart was hollow and her nests empty.

Paradox

Making connections is more than effective strategy, one means to the end of arresting, memorable writing; it is also its own substance, an end in itself. It proclaims the imagination to be not only alive and active but also crucial to the apprehension of truth. Imaginative vision is democratic, inclusive, unsqueamish, willing to see life steadily and whole. It is the birthplace of *paradox,* the "deathplace" of propaganda, which pushes a single truth and dumps everything else.

Literature handbooks define *paradox* as "an *apparent* contradiction," thereby diminishing the figure of speech that all other figures move toward, the mode of expression that heightens tension to the utmost and comes closest to capturing the *real* complexity of truth. Rogers's poem "The Family Is All There Is" springs from a single grand metaphor of global "family ties" and resemblances. Yet the eccentric particularity of each image strains against the premise of common ancestry; the poem embodies the paradox of unity in diversity, the idea that the many are one. In Kunitz's poem "Indian Summer at Land's End," the images play on the tension between permanence and change, the temporary and the timeless, subsuming these antitheses in two images of "permanent change": the ocean and the victorious, ever-migrating geese. In Hughes's "Harlem," the past festers in the present and finally destroys the future, as images of passive suffering give way to active life/death, when the deferred dream explodes in militancy. Haines's "Green Man" of spring and renewed life brings so much mess and chaos that "the valley shudders" at his arrival.

Despite the insistence of our Western logic that opposites are not allowed to coexist, every person on the street knows that opposites attract and cling to each other. In fact, it seems sometimes that paradox defines the dynamic of our psychic lives, in which feelings and attitudes are always competing with and toppling into their "opposites." As William Blake reminded us two centuries ago, "Excess of sorrow laughs. Excess of joy weeps." And "if the fool would persist in his folly he would become wise."

NOTEBOOK OPTIONS

1. We are all bundles of contradictions. We are often torn between head and heart, responsibility and spontaneity, or that most awful quandary, mercy and justice. Most of us have sympathy for more than one interest group or ideology; in our day-to-day behavior, we are always crossing party lines.

   List some of the different competing ideologies and values that you would like to live by. Choose two and personify them, one as a male and one as a female, but if you feel gender stereotypes tugging you one way, you can simply change the sex of your characters. Give them names; describe them physically; imagine their strengths, weaknesses, jobs, hobbies. What kind of books does each read? What music does each listen to? Imagine the two of them marrying. What would the bride wear? Who would be in the wedding party? Describe the ceremony and/or a scene from the reception.

2. In Western literature, it has become commonplace to play on the connections between religion, romance, and warfare. Love is "a campaign"; war is "sacred"; faith is "a battle" or "a marriage". Make a list of activities, more specific and personal than these three age-old conventionalized ones, activities you enjoy or at which you are proficient. Playing a hunch as to their possibilities, select two activities from this list and try to describe the process of one (A) in terms of the other (B). (Could playing tennis be like planting a garden? Could dancing be like a debate? Could developing a photograph be like reading a book?) Before you begin, you might want to make two other lists, one of the important steps in (A) and one of the tools and terms associated with

(B). Alternatively, select one of these activities and describe an episode in a relationship (parent and child, siblings, boss and employee, partners, husband and wife) in terms of the activity.

3. Look back over your list of abstractions and your list of objects from the last exercise in Chapter 7: Showing versus Telling. Select one item from either list, and write its autobiography. Pay attention to the circumstances of the item's birth and then three or four stages in its life. For example, consider the following: What would the childhood of pollution be like? The adolescence of a parking meter?

4. As Chapter 2: Working with Words pointed out, adverbs often weaken the verbs or adjectives they were meant to intensify. Yet beginning writers, striving for vividness and precision, often find adverbs irresistible. The following is a way you can eliminate unnecessary adverbs from your writing and add to its concreteness and imaginative energy.

   Choose a passage from your notebook that contains a number of *-ly* adverbs. Think of each one as an unfinished simile—the *-ly* suffix derives, after all, from the word *like*. Experiment with different ways of completing the simile, and see if one of them won't serve in place of the adverb. For example:

> He scanned the room nervously. . . . nervous as a mouse in captivity . . .
> He scanned the room like a captive mouse.
>
> He wiped the baby's face skillfully. . . . skillful as a jeweler . . . A jeweler with a many-faceted gem, he wiped every bit of mashed potatoes from the baby's face and head.

Chapter 9

Choosing a Point of View

We only see what we look at. To look is an act of choice.
John Berger, *Ways of Seeing*

Where are all these observations coming from? We can't assume the answer is quick and simple: "Why, from me. These observations are my images, my words." Even in the most personal essay or poem, as we begin to work with our material, further questions arise: Well, who am I in this piece of writing, what position am I taking? Why am I choosing to look at what I see? What's my perspective, my angle on it, my distance from it? How much do I know? What would I rather not have to know? Early in the process of shaping a finished product, we begin to answer these questions. Whether by unconscious choice, deliberate device, or intuition, as we go along we always wind up creating a writing self along with the writing. The perspective we take, the point of view we select, the persona or narrator we create, the voice we sustain—all are powerful determinants of the final work.

Perspectives

All observation implies a vantage point or perspective. When as writers we choose an angle on our subject matter and establish our distance from it, when we decide which details to emphasize and which to consign to background, we are creating a perspective. Simple shifts in *perspective* can prompt magical transformations. An object or activity we have always taken for granted may reveal intriguing "hidden" characteristics when removed from its normal context or regarded from an unusual angle or an unexpected distance. Characters show surprising dimensions; atmosphere changes. The issue of perspective is most obviously crucial to fiction, where it defines narrative point of view and establishes who will tell the tale. Yet in their search for original perspectives, writers have created a much wider array of options than those associated with point of view in fiction, options that work in poems and essays as well.

The following poem, "Childhood," by Maura Stanton, brings to remembering an imaginative shift in perspective and thus creates an original metaphor, first, for a young girl's disappointment with her family and, later, as her playful escape from its shabby reality becomes habit, for a more encompassing sense of dislocation.

I used to lie on my back, imagining
A reverse house on the ceiling of my house
Where I could walk around in empty rooms
All by myself. There was no furniture
Up there, only a glass globe in the floor,
And knee-high barriers at every door.
The low silled windows opened on blue air.
Nothing hung in the closet; even the kitchen
Seemed immaculate, a place for thought.
I liked to walk across the swirling plaster
Into the parts of the house I couldn't see.
The hum from the other house, now my ceiling
Reached me only faintly. I'd look up
To find my brothers watching old cartoons,
Or my mother vacuuming the ugly carpet.
I'd stare amazed at unmade beds, the clutter,
Shoes, half-dressed dolls, the telephone,
Then return dizzily to my perfect floorplan
Where I never spoke or listened to anyone.
I must have turned down the wrong hall,
Or opened a door that locked shut behind me,
For I live on the ceiling now, not the floor.
This is my house, room after empty room.
How do I ever get back to the real house
Where my sisters spill milk, my father calls,
And I am at the table, eating cereal?
I fill my white rooms with furniture,
Hang curtains over the piercing blue outside.
I lie on my back. I strive to look down,
This ceiling is higher than it used to be,
The floor so far away I can't determine
Which room I'm in, which year, which life.

What we see is determined not only by our angle on our subject (as in Stanton's creative headstand above) but also by our distance from it. Our fellow humans appear one way when we gaze down on them from the top of the Washington Monument, another way when we are driving the loop from the National Air and Space Museum to the Lincoln Memorial in a failed quest for a parking space. A flower shows a larger, more detailed face to a hummingbird than it does to a human being strolling through the garden.

Halfway through his essay "The Iks," Lewis Thomas steps back from an African tribe whose mean and loveless behavior (they desert their children and old people and laugh at each other's misfortunes) he has been describing. From a distance, he sees a shocking resemblance between the individual Ik, a representative of raw, uncivilized human nature, and modern, civilized humans as they behave in groups.

> Cities have all the Ik characteristics. They defecate on doorsteps, in rivers and lakes, their own or anyone else's. They leave rubbish. They detest all neighboring cities, give nothing away. They even build institutions for deserting elders out of sight.
>
> Nations are the most Ik-like of all. . . . For total greed, rapacity, heartlessness, and irresponsibility there is nothing to match a nation. Nations, by law, are solitary, self-centered, withdrawn into themselves. There is no such thing as affection between nations, and certainly no nation ever loved another. They bawl insults from their doorsteps, defecate into whole oceans, snatch all the food, survive by detestation, take joy in the bad luck of others, celebrate the death of others, live for the death of others.

EXERCISE: From an Alien Perspective

Call to mind an activity or routine with which you are familiar, and describe it from the point of view of an uninitiated outsider—a visiting alien from another planet; a member of a distant, "primitive" culture who has somehow washed up in the Western world; or a person from a past century somehow catapulted into ours.

There is no need to account for the circumstances of your visitor's arrival, or for the fact that she or he speaks English. But you may employ your visitor's grasp of English to reflect her or his background. If so, what limits does this background impose on your language? In what other ways does this radically innocent/ignorant point of view constrain what you can say? As you share your writing with your group, be attentive to those passages that most imaginatively maintain the perspective and those passages in which the perspective seems to waver. You will probably find many of these descriptions funny. Where is the comedy coming from? Notice that your visitor's (mis)interpretations often result from his or her failure to understand the "proper" angle or distance from which your activity is supposed to be observed.

•   •   •

The perspective of the innocent/ignorant outsider has served writers of comedy and satire for centuries. We see it working whenever the "country" boy or girl hits the big city, or whenever adult activities and conventions are reflected through the perspective of a young child. The gains are many. There's the surprise in viewing life without our often sacred cultural assumptions: imagine how the rituals of a church service would look to someone who hasn't been taught what she or he is supposed to feel during them. There's the comedy or poignancy of misunderstanding: imagine a sexual encounter described as a death struggle or a boxing match as a dance of desire; imagine a child fantasizing in vain against the facts of poverty. There is always tension, and there is always the opportunity for moral comment: the clash between the explicit "odd" perspective and the implicit "normal" one provokes us to reassess our assumptions. As with the child in Anderson's fairy tale who was just unsophisticated enough to call the emperor naked, the naïve point of view may bring us closer to truth.

A radically limited perspective can open up a subject with provocative new material. As you may have discovered, however, limits can also become drawbacks in an extended piece of writing. A limited perspective simplifies complexity, reducing a process to disconnected steps, an idea to simple facts. It tends toward the deadpan, and thus suppresses emotion. It restricts the writer's play with the most basic resource—language. On the other hand, restrictions may offer a productive security. The more a chosen perspective imposes limits, the more the writer begins to feel that the work is writing itself, and that can be a pleasant feeling. In the case of the child's perspective, story writers and essayists smoothly get around its disadvantages by adding another mirror: the grown-up looking back, who reflects and interprets the behavior of the young child trying to reflect the behavior of the grown-up world.

EXERCISE: First Memory

In his famous opening to *Portrait of the Artist as a Young Man*, the modern Irish writer James Joyce assembles the fragments of his protagonist's earliest memories:

Once upon a time and a very good time it was there was a moocow coming down along the road and this moocow that was down along the road met a nicens little boy named baby tuckoo. . . .

His father told him that story: his father looked at him through a glass: he had a hairy face.

He was baby tuckoo. The moocow came down the road where Betty Byrne lived: she sold lemon platt. . . .

When you wet the bed, first it is warm then it gets cold. His mother put on the oilsheet. That had the queer smell.

His mother had a nicer smell than his father. She played on the piano the sailor's hornpipe for him to dance.

Recall and record your own earliest, probably composite memory, trying to simulate through word choice and syntax the perspective of a young child. Draft these memories in the first person and the present tense. Notice in Joyce's opening how important raw sensory perceptions are, particularly the more "primal" senses of touch, taste, smell in rendering the world as perceived by an undeveloped mind.

Now try to bring your adult perspective to bear on this early experience. Writing in the past tense, with the benefit of greater knowledge, recast this memory. In what ways does the raw naïveté of a child bring freshness to the description/narration? In what ways does hindsight and more sophisticated thinking enrich it? Can you imagine achieving a balance in perspective that would allow you the best of both worlds?

Narrative Point of View

One aspect of perspective has tended to invite systematic analysis more than most other elements of creative writing. Like the form of the sonnet, or rhetorical models for the essay, the basic options for *narrative point of view* make a scheme our intellects can grasp and fiddle with. Unfortunately, as with the Shakespearean sonnet or the comparison-contrast essay, the mastery of a technical scheme doesn't guarantee dynamic, meaningful writing.

Yet point of view (unlike a rhyme scheme or a formal outline) exists as soon as we put words on a page, whether we mean it to or not. As literary critics have realized, point of view is much more than a technical strategy superimposed on the story material; it grows out of the story material and *creates* the story; in a sense, it *is* the story. Thus some knowledge of how its basic options tend to work helps us make educated guesses as to what might be the most inspiring, fruitful point of view to take at the start of a narrative, as well as what intermediate problems a revision of point of view might solve.

Narrative points of view divide broadly into two groups: those that establish themselves somewhere inside the created world and speak in the *first person*, and those outside it, whether one small step removed or many, that speak in the *third person*. In the latter group, variations in distance and insight tend to cluster around three possibilities: total omniscience, limited omniscience, and fly-on-the-wall. In the case of *total omniscience*, the narrator is presumed to have access to all information about the world of the narrative: its past, present, and even future; the inner lives of all its characters; its action *here* and its action *there* ("back at the ranch . . ."). In the case of *limited omniscience*, a nameless narrator is established just outside the fictional world, hovering over the main character, whose story is told in the third person. The story may reveal *everything* about a single character, but logistically, no happenings can enter the story except through the perception of this character; what the main character isn't in on, the reader can't be in on. When the point of view is that of a *fly on the wall*, the narrative covers all the characters in all locales but is barred from exploring or guessing at their inner lives. In other words, it covers external behavior in the neutral, factual way an indifferent fly on the wall might witness it.

First Person

Where narrative point of view is concerned, there is safety in limitation. Total omniscience means choosing an appropriate distance, focus, and direction out of all possible distances, foci, and directions. It means determining what might be necessary or fertile information among an infinity of potential data. Such freedom can be overwhelming. The best bet for the inexperienced story writer is to begin by experimenting with the *first-person point of view*. This choice doesn't necessarily mean asking the central character to narrate and explain his or her own actions. In a variation on the first-person point of view, the "I" takes a position off to one side of the main action and offers commentary as witness to the central character or characters. This arrangement is particularly apt when the central character must remain mysterious, somehow inexplicable (think of Catherine and Heathcliff in Emily Brontë's *Wuthering Heights* or F. Scott Fitzgerald's *Great Gatsby* or the sociopathic McMurphy in Ken Kesey's *One Flew over the Cockoo's Nest*, all of whom are observed by first-person "witnesses"). Often when writers choose the perspective of a young child to describe the adult world, an "I-as-witness" emerges, peripheral, puzzled, powerless.

The first-person point of view can require some ingenuity for gaining access to other characters' inner lives, as well as to events the narrator hasn't witnessed. But there is one decided advantage to this choice: it generates credibility almost automatically. For one thing, an "I" engages readers immediately and arouses their curiosity often in spite of themselves. For another, it bestows authority—it is more plausible that the "I" narrator should have fairly complete, intimate information about the attitudes and experiences of the "I" character and what is going on around him or her. In third-person narration, on the other hand, readers must be made to believe that some nameless voice speaks such information about someone else, or about a whole group of someone elses.

Perhaps most important, first-person narration forces the writer to get inside the main character and his or her created world, to ask questions—What is happening to me at this particular moment? Why am I doing this?—and to imagine all the surrounding details that a more distant third-person narrator might neglect. In other words, choosing first- rather than third-person point of view often serves to open up a narrative and get below its surface.

EXERCISE: Getting Inside the First Person

Choose one of the biographical portraits of a relative you created in Chapter 4: Remembering. Try recomposing it in the first person from the point of view of that relative. Use the following guidelines: allow your character to offer a physical self-description (perhaps proudly, apologetically, or jokingly,); allow him or her to give a sketch and opinion of *you;* focus on one of his or her actions mentioned in the original portrait and offer an explanation of this action or perhaps even an apology for it.

Do you find yourself prompted to say more than you did in the original portrait? Are you more aware of gaps in the picture that need filling in? How does his or her commentary on an action differ from yours? Might he or she bring up material you neglected to mention about his or her past?

Limited Omniscience

Many contemporary fiction writers choose the *third-person limited omniscient point of view* because it combines the focus and depth of first-person narration with a greater flexibility in language, image, and also distance. Just as the narrator is not as strictly confined to the linguistic resources of his or her main character, the narrator can articulate insights of which his or her character may be only vaguely aware. In the following opening from the story "Zoe," by Molly Best Tinsley, limited omniscience explains the social strategy of a troubled fifteen-year-old:

> She liked to be the first to speak. It wasn't that she wanted to be nice, put them at ease; it was her way of warning them not to be, of setting the tone she did best: bemused, even ironic, but formal. She didn't want any of them thinking she was someone to cultivate. Whenever those voices, low and strained, interrupted her life downstairs, whether they came late at night from the front hall or mornings from the kitchen, she slipped into the one-piece camouflage suit she used as a bathrobe, wrapped the belt twice around her slim waist, and ascended to meet her mother's latest. She liked to catch him with breakfast in his mouth, or romance on his mind, and then before he could compose himself, she announced, "I am Zoe, her daughter," offering a little bow and a graceful hand, limp as a spray of japonica.

Reread this passage, trying in your mind both to translate it into the first person and to hear how it would sound that way. (This mental conversion is a handy, labor-saving skill worth practicing for future experiments with point of view.) How does the tone of the passage change if you allow Zoe herself to explain her behavior? What is gained by the indirection and slight distance? Can you imagine some of the problems that might arise if, on the other hand, you opted for even more distance and complete omniscience for your narrator? In considering complete omniscience, think about what you construe about Zoe's situation thus far. Suppose this situation were described explicitly, right up front, as full omniscience would tend to require? What would be the effect?

Fly on the Wall

The second limited point of view among the third-person options has been variously called *fly-on-the-wall*, *dramatic*, and *cinematic*. Although this point of view does not confine itself to the experience of a single character, it shoots for complete neutrality in describing setting and narrating behavior. It can vary angle and distance the way a camera can, but like a camera, it never penetrates surfaces. In fact, it is *showing* in its

purest, perhaps most challenging, form. Things and their positions, action, and dialogue are the pared-down resources with which the cinematic
narrator illustrates but never tells what is meant.

The following is a passage of dramatic narration from Dashiell Ham-
mett's *Maltese Falcon*. Why would this cinematic, "objective" point of
view be perfectly suited to a detective novel?

> Spade sank into his swivel-chair, made a quarter-turn to face her,
> smiled politely. He smiled without separating his lips. All the V's in
> his face grew longer. . . . Somewhere in a neighboring office a
> power-driven machine vibrated dully. On Spade's desk a limp ciga-
> rette smoldered in a brass tray filled with the remains of limp ciga-
> rettes. Ragged grey flakes of cigarette-ash dotted the yellow top of the
> desk and the green blotter and the papers that were there. A buff-
> curtained window, eight or ten inches open, let in from the court a
> current of air faintly scented with ammonia. The ashes on the desk
> twitched and crawled in the current.
>
> Miss Wonderly watched the grey flakes twitch and crawl. Her eyes
> were uneasy. She sat on the very edge of her chair. Her feet were flat
> on the floor, as if she were about to rise.

Notice the range of sensory images and their capacity to *show* the
sordid, shady world Sam Spade inhabits. How much does the close rendering of things and behavior suggest in the way of ideas and feelings?

Pronouns in the Poem and Essay

Where credibility and authority are concerned, the poet faces almost the opposite problem from that faced by the writer of fiction. Too
few readers *doubt* that the poet speaks personal truths straight from the
heart, and the general assumption, that the poet is confessing sincerely,
can actually deaden curiosity. To jolt readers out of these old assumptions
about the self-centered lyric, contemporary poets often test other pronouns, accosting readers with *you* or gently including them with *we*.

In some poems, the *you* will be the general *you*, working to objectify
or universalize the experience transcribed. In other cases, the speaker
addresses the subject of the poem in the second person instead of describing him, her, or it in the third person. The effect is to turn what might
have been a portrait into a sort of one-sided conversation.

In the poem "Simple-song," by Marge Piercy, the pronoun *we* brings
a new perspective to what might have been just another personal love
poem about the pain and frustration of loss. Try to imagine it in an earlier
stage, a notebook jotting in the *I* form.

When we are going toward someone we say
you are just like me
your thoughts are my brothers
word matches word
how easy to be together.

When we are leaving someone we say
how strange you are
we cannot communicate
we can never agree
how hard, hard and weary to be together.

We are not different nor alike
but each strange in his leather body
sealed in skin and reaching out clumsy hands
and loving is an act
that cannot outlive
the open hand
the open eye
the door in the chest standing open.

We in a poem may lend a mysterious, almost omniscient resonance to the speaker's voice, yet in an essay seem perfectly conventional, and even evasive. Similarly, *you* in a poem may induce engagement and curiosity, but in an essay sound too presumptuous, too preachy, or too smacking of process analysis. It may actually separate writer from audience too insistently. The most reliably effective and honest point of view for the essay remains the *I*, its original focus. It is unfortunate that beginning writers are still being advised to avoid it, in favor of the formal *one*, the passive voice, and other roundabout expressions, for the *I* in all its subjectivity is the reason and energy behind the creative essay.

EXERCISE: Changing Pronouns

Find a passage in your notebook that seems highly personal in content, perhaps even confessional. Experiment by changing the *I* to *you* or *we*: read the passage aloud to yourself, transposing the pronouns as you go along. Can you hear the shift to a different pronoun give your material an "edge," just the right kind of strangeness, perhaps, to inspire new developments?

Persona

By *the help of an image*
I call to my own opposite, summon all
That I have handled least, least looked upon.

William Butler Yeats, "Ego Dominus Tuus"

Point of view is first a geographical matter, having to do with where you stand in relation to your material. Once determined, this vantage point may begin to develop a psychological dimension, as some of the preceding examples have already suggested. In other words, point of view often gives birth to an identifiable *persona* (or speaker) with particular attributes in particular surroundings.

In the dramatic monologues of Victorian poet Robert Browning persona becomes the central issue. In the course of each monologue Browning creates a morally ambiguous character, imagines him at a specific moment of crisis in his life, and allows him to reveal himself and his situation. By speaking through these personae—hypocrites, rogues, even psychopathic murderers—Browning dramatizes the ironies and complexities of human behavior. Thus in his well-known "My Last Duchess," we catch an elegant aristocrat of the Italian Renaissance in the act of explaining the portrait of his deceased wife to an emissary from the father of his new wife-to-be. We infer with growing horror that the duke has had this first wife murdered because her warm, spontaneous gregariousness threatened his rigid control.

EXERCISE: Choosing an Alter Ego

Try inventing a persona for yourself. You might begin by imagining an *alter ego*, someone you may have daydreamed about being, someone with the nerve to do things you would never do, say things you can never think to say. How might you embody this fantasy self? Consider variables such as gender, age, race, religion, occupation; try a surprising combination. Make a list of further attributes (favorite foods, colors, music, pastimes, verbal expressions; strengths and weaknesses; politics; family background). You may be aware of more than one figure lurking, lounging, preening, in different corners of your mind. Try to get each one defined in concrete images and specific attributes. These portraits are always open; further details may come to you weeks from now; add them to the lists.

Now select a piece of descriptive or anecdotal writing from your notebook. Imagine one of your personae reading it and telling you that it is wrong—not exactly false, not a deliberate lie, but definitely the wrong emphasis, the wrong impression. Let your persona present his or her version of the way it was.

• • •

Notice that telling becomes a way of showing when you deliberately create the teller. In other words, if your persona makes sweeping general statements or is given to abstract rambling, these habits distinguish him or her as a character; they are showing your reader what your persona is like.

Voice

Sentences are not different enough to hold the attention unless they are dramatic. . . . All that can save them is the speaking tone of voice somehow entangled in the words and fastened to the page for the ear of the imagination.

Robert Frost, Introduction, *A Way Out*

Every piece of writing is, to varying degrees, a dramatic monologue whose distinctive, dynamic voice can exert a powerful hold on the reader. Even the deliberately neutral fly-on-the-wall point of view creates a voice—one that is detached, factual, restrained. More often, strong writing reproduces a voice speaking intensely on its subject, energized by a problematic occasion, a specific audience, and/or a purpose. In writing where voice is at work it is the complicated *occasion* that seems to dictate what gets said and what makes the words resound audibly for the reader.

Voice is an elusive quality to define in writing, and yet it may be the very source of coherence in a finished work. Writers talk of revision after revision, tossing countless manuscript pages into the trash, in pursuit of the right voice. Those who tend toward cynicism about the possibility of *learning* creative writing throw up their hands at the issue of voice and sigh that you either have it or you don't.

Whether we are trying to find our own singular voice, the voice of a created narrator, or simply the voice of a particular essay or poem, the first condition for success seems to be a relaxed, spontaneous frame of mind, free from judgment—this at a time when the effort to write may be causing just the opposite: anxiety, overthinking, self-criticism. Imagine that you telephone an acquaintance with some important information to convey and have to deliver the message into an answering machine. When you first start speaking, your voice is stiff and unnatural, full of awkward hesitation. Yet if the message is long enough, you might find yourself warming to the one-sided conversation. Your natural voice takes over, animated and fluent. Of course, when you are having a "live" talk with a friend in a relaxed setting, chances are your voice is free the whole time—free to become its fluent, flexible self, responsive to both audience and subject.

In the following passage, a student looks at her world from the point of view of her cat. At first, this appears to be a response to an assignment: the sentences are stiff; some ideas hit, others miss. Then, gradually, the writer seems to fall under the spell of her subject, and a live voice bursts onto the page.

> The Belly-petter pushes the cleaning machine across the floor, wailing songs from Camelot. They are no match for the lovely music I make outside at midnight with the other True Beings. She dares to move me from my comfy padded rest. She belts "What the Simple Folk Do." What she calls simple, I call simply stupid. They whistle, they sing, they dance. They don't think to just stop, rub their cheeks against a door, and lick a paw. *That's* simple.
>
> Now the roaring fur-sucker chases me from my sunspot on the carpet, then the Belly-petter stops to flutter and flick the dust off tables and shelves. Relax, pale child. Find a warm place and stretch your haunches. Sink into your body and feel the pleasure of a purr.
>
> Rachelle Smith

When we stop being aware that we are writing, voice can take over. In the meantime, we can strengthen voice by practicing voices—imagining specific occasions for our writing and stretching, coloring, shaping it accordingly. Consider that we humans speak out of need. We want something that we cannot get by keeping silent, whether that something be as concrete as the salt at the other end of the table or as intangible as approval. We want money, food, jobs, clothes, cars, knowledge, respect, sex, affection, punishment, forgiveness. These are our ends to which speech serves as a supple, versatile means. We beg, cajole, boast, seduce, invite, insult, lambast, confess, aware all the while of our audience, which may or may not be willing to grant what we ask.

EXERCISE: Writing As a Speech Act

Read the following short "voice poem" by William Carlos Williams aloud, emphasizing the rhythm and inflection that these words seem to call for.

This Is Just to Say

I have eaten
the plums
that were in
the ice box

and which
you were probably
saving
for breakfast

Forgive me
they were delicious
so sweet
and so cold

Note that these carefully arranged words simulate a speech act, that of apology. What is it in the words and their ordering that creates the apologetic voice? Try a loose imitation of this speech act, in a paragraph or so, adapting it to an event in your own life, imagining the specific audience and his or her probable response. You don't have to restrain yourself to an explanation as brief as Williams's poem. What sort of verbal twists and turns might you take to get around your audience's disapproval? Notice even blunt honesty is a sort of strategy here.

•   •   •

To approach voice in a piece of writing, think of writing as a *speech act*, or strategy, with an occasion, an audience, and a purpose. The act isn't always as simple and single-dimensional as an apology or a reprimand, but it is generated by some need. Study carefully the opening paragraphs of the stories and essays you read and the opening lines of poems. Try to identify the strategies behind the distinctive voices that hook the reader into continuing. Following are the first two sentences gleaned from five different prize-winning stories from *Best American Short Stories 1984* and *Best American Short Stories 1985*.

> To begin, then, here is a scene in which I am the man and my friend Sarah Cole is the woman. I don't mind describing it now, because I'm a decade older and don't look the same now as I did then, and Sarah is dead.
>
> Russell Banks, "Sarah Cole: A Type of Love Story"

> Let me tell you who I am. I'm sixty-nine years old, live in the same house I was raised in, and have been the high school biology

and astronomy teacher in this town so long that I have taught the grandson of one of my former students.

> Ethan Canin, "Emperor of the Air"

I am twenty-seven: three weeks ago a black Great Dane stalked into my classroom as I was passing out theme topics. My students turned about to look.

> Michael Bishop, "Dogs' Lives"

The name's John Q. Slade. I'm a talk show host.

> Bev Jafek, "You've Come a Long Way, Mickey Mouse"

My name is Luke Ripley, and here is what I call my life: I own a stable of thirty horses, and I have young people who teach riding, and we board some horses too. This is in northeastern Massachusetts.

> Andre Dubus, "A Father's Story"

Taken alone, each might seem to be a simple, straightforward introduction, unworthy of particular notice. All exemplify the same first-person point of view, but with such variations. Look carefully at the different strategies, revealed in diction and imagery as well as in syntax, and you begin to appreciate the amazing economy with which each writer establishes a voice.

NOTEBOOK OPTIONS

1. Describe a setting in your hometown, including in your description only objects bigger than a car (the sky, literally, is the limit). Then describe the same locale including only objects smaller than a car.
2. Return to your childhood enemy of Chapter 4: Remembering and to the scene of his or her crime(s). Give an account of the scene from his or her point of view. Would the confrontation lend itself to presentation by a fly on the wall—or perhaps a hawk flying overhead? What would be lost? Would anything be gained?
3. Recall a recent happening in your life that embarrassed or angered you (or simply a condition of your current life that provokes the same reaction). Compose three full versions of the event or condition—one from your point of view, one from the point of view of a specific outsider (a bus driver, a homeless person in the bus station), and one in the third-person omniscient point of view. What restrictions did you instinctively impose on the total omniscience of the third version? Notice that certain subjective concerns of each first-person narrator

may interfere with his or her objectivity. Try to capture these differences in agenda through voice, as well as through point of view.

4. Return to the list of abstractions you accumulated in Chapter 7: Showing versus Telling. Add to it any additional abstract concepts that
come to mind, then compose a brief speech including as many of them
as you can. What persona does this speech imply?

5. "Perform" in writing one of the following speech acts (or one of your
own choice) by relating it to an issue in your current life: confessing,
commanding, scolding, promising. Who will be your audience (a po-
lice officer, a lover, a parent, a child)? What is it that you want from
the confrontation, and why is he or she withholding it? Try at least to
imply this information in your speech. For practice, exaggerate the
particular quality of the voice—the pathos or cunning or arrogance or
disgust.

6. Reread the material you generated for your dream city in Chapter 5:
Dreaming. Try to reconceive the description in a new, purposeful
voice. Perhaps the voice is keeping alive a memory; perhaps it is selling
real estate; perhaps it is scandal-mongering. In any case, who would be
the probable audience?

PART THREE

Developing Form

Chapter 10

Shaping

*The pen works for itself, and acts like a hand, modeling the
plastic material over and over again to the form that suits it best.
The form is never arbitrary, but is a sort of growth like crys-
tallization, as any artist knows too well; for often the pencil or
pen runs into side-paths and shapelessness, loses its relations,
stops or is bogged. Then it has to return on its trail, and recover,
if it can, its line of force.*

Henry Adams, The Education of Henry Adams

Most contemporary writers, echoing the claims of early nineteenth-
century Romantic poets, view harmony, balance, order, and movement
(aspects of form) as qualities of a work of art they *uncover* or *reveal* as they
struggle to represent a particular subject, rather than as qualities that they
impose from outside or that come ready-made. Samuel Taylor Coleridge
clearly articulated this natural interconnection between form and content:

> The organic form . . . is innate; it shapes, as it develops, itself from
> within, and the fullness of its development is one and the same with
> the perfection of its outward form.

Coleridge, William Wordsworth, William Blake, and others replaced the
Classical model of writer as imitator with the Romantic one of writer (or
any artist) as discoverer, an aesthetic doctrine that persists today. According to contemporary poet Denise Levertov:

> Form is never more than a revelation of content. . . . There is form
> in all things (and in our experience) which the poet can discover and
> reveal.

A complicated process, the discovery of form demands of the writer
a shifting back and forth between speculation and reflection. So far, this

book has suggested two stages to the writing process: the first stage intuitive, inventive, and speculative (concerned more with the parts than the whole); the second reflective, judgmental, and reasoned (preoccupied with the order and coherence of the whole). The writer first generates, and then refines. In practice, however, writing does not always move in one direction (from expansion to contraction); the writer often shifts back and forth from speculation to judgment to speculation: from invention to revision to invention.

Expansion and Contraction

A good deal of shaping is intuitive, done "by feel," according to William Stafford, not "by rule." Sometimes in the process of writing, you will discover an action so strong it seems to dictate a new direction for a story, a stanza so luminous it shines more vividly than any other, a paragraph so apparently seamless it makes the others in the essay appear clumsy and forced. If your intuition tells you that one part of a poem, a story, or an essay in progress eclipses the whole, trust that it will take you somewhere interesting. Follow the lead of a brilliant passage, a dazzling line, or a particularly interesting character; learn to look for the jewel hidden in the larger, rambling draft and to be willing to sacrifice an original conception to something invented seemingly by accident. If, in working on a poem about your sister's flightiness and irresponsibility, for example, you notice that the most interesting part of the poem describes her crazy outfits, then put aside the initial intent momentarily and ride the crest of that wave with descriptions of her zany getups. If such a creative departure turns out to be a productive one, which it often will, and threatens to overwhelm your initial plan, let it. Initial schemes are often too vast and unwieldy anyway. A painter once remarked that when she'd finished a five-foot by five-foot canvas, she'd find the one square foot of it that interested her the most and "blow up" just that portion by transferring it to a much larger canvas.

Following a creative impulse or building on the strong parts of a work-in-progress is not the same as requiring yourself to perfect one section before going on to the next. On a first draft, don't stop a page into a story in order to perfect the beginning before advancing any further. The same caution holds for the first stanza of a poem or the introductory paragraph of an essay. Such preoccupation with perfecting a given part will too often inhibit the spontaneity necessary to generate more parts (and finally the whole) and will lead inevitably to frustration. As this book has stressed earlier, you need to risk clumsiness and banality in generating as complete a rough draft as possible, the zero-draft.

Ultimately an inefficient process, writing demands excess, the willingness on the part of the writer to generate far more ideas, pages, lines, or paragraphs than will ever appear in the finished product; to experiment with alternative ways of telling; and to collect data in support of every generalization. The zero-draft will certainly be flabby in some parts and scanty in others but will, at least, contain the main ingredients of the piece. When you're composing the zero-draft, remember that eliminating excess is generally easier than building from scratch, so write knowing that there will be waste. You'll be surprised how liberating that can be.

At times during the drafting process, and then finally at the completion of the zero-draft, step back from the work in progress and search for what may appear only as a faint hint of pattern and design. Build on that nascent design; exploit it. When composing lines of a poem, note the possibility of images and sounds that echo one another. In looking over the draft of an essay, assess how the middle and the end advance the point let loose at the beginning. When developing a character, ask if a single gesture, statement, or action might form the basis of a trait. Remember that telling a story is more than sequencing events; it requires an element of suspense. Through the delicate deployment of images and metaphors as instruments of foreshadowing you can enhance suspense. Or to whet your reader's curiosity, your narrator might comment, "I could tell something was about to happen," or "She had never said anything like that before." Similarly, once you have a sense of where a narrative is going, how it will conclude itself, you can revise earlier portions to introduce hints of this conclusion.

A general rule of painters—if you want your viewer to see something (brush stroke, line, or color) you need to repeat it three times in the same work—pertains as well to writing. One allusion to a quality, feeling, idea, or image may go unnoticed by the reader; two references is a coincidence; three a pattern. A pattern of associations not only underscores a theme but also helps draw the various parts of your story, essay, or poem together. Burgundy velvet curtains in one part of a story, a tight, red silk dress in another, and a crimson sky can establish a reverberation that won't rescue a poor piece of writing but will strengthen a good one. In the small room of the poem, this repetition with a slight difference, this echoing of images and sounds, is essential.

Shaping often demands that the writer expand parts and focus the whole. Beginning writers frequently extend the drama of their stories over the course of several weeks or months, when one day might forcefully center their conflicts. A poet who shifts from one scene, one mood, or one character to another might better concentrate on a single scene, mood or character. The essayist who begins by writing about teenage girls and their cars may do well to narrow the essay to one or two specific examples.

Advancing the Whole

So far this discussion of shaping has centered on recognizing patterns within a draft. What about the overarching pattern of the whole work? Having finished the zero-draft of a story, ask yourself where you've gone and where you've taken your characters. Could you say that a character passes from innocence to experience, ignorance to insight, from isolation to incorporation (or vice versa)? In what different way would you like the reader to see a character, an action, a place, an object, the speaker in a poem, or the subject of an essay by the end of the piece? If you set up an opposition in a poem, an essay, or a story, how do you resolve it?

This book assumes that we often lack such a grand structure at the beginning of our writing and that in the process of writing we discover the possibility of a work's shape and scope.

EXERCISE: Alternative Structures

One of the most fundamental movements in literature is the movement from disequilibrium to equilibrium. Even the idyllic world of the fairy tale—which opens on the paradisal kingdom, the birth of a beautiful princess, or the coming to manhood of a handsome prince—within the first few paragraphs typically suffers a disturbance (abduction, death, or challenge that must be met). In contemporary literature, disturbance may reveal itself more subtly, in the struggles of a character (or speaker of a poem) to make sense of an event or in the juxtaposition of discordant images.

Select a story, a poem, or an essay in progress in which a character or the speaker is grappling with something that is not right, not resolved. Propose four alternative resolutions. How does each one change what your work-in-progress is about? Do certain resolutions require deletions or expansions of material in the middle, in order to shift emphasis and adequately prepare for the ending? Take as a ridiculous example Little Red Riding Hood's encounter with the wolf. Think about the different themes proposed by each of the following conclusions:

Seeing a large stone beside her on the path and sensing imminent danger, Red Riding Hood takes care of the varmint right then and there.

For weeks afterward, the little girl carries on a secret relationship with the wolf, meeting him on the path each day, sharing goodies intended for grandmother, and finally skipping school to hang out with him.

While sitting alone on her porch one night, Red Riding Hood's mournful mother sees the ghost of her daughter, angelic in her crimson cape, who reassures her mother that she is happy in heaven.

Red Riding Hood, having been told repeatedly never to talk to strangers on the path, runs ahead of the wolf down the path. Had she not dropped the basket of Grandma's food, the wolf would surely have caught up with her. Luckily, he stops to eat the food (a more certain catch than a spunky little girl), and she makes it to the cottage before the wolf.

• • •

One of the most common structures in literature is the *journey*, in which the main character or the narrator sets out on a literal or metaphoric (psychological) journey, one often filled with obstacles. The overcoming of such obstacles transforms the main character from youth to adult, from sinner to saint, or from naïve individual to wise person. At its grandest, the epic journey sets into operation three worlds at once— heaven, earth, and the underworld—and charts the circular passage of hero through physical hardships and mental tribulations to a new world order or the restoration of the old. Though probably not on so vast a scale, your own fiction may chart a journey, maybe one from ignorance to insight or from confusion to clarity.

Like stories, many poems and essays unfold along narrative lines. Some, however, establish contrasts (of present and past, of inside and outside, of what things seem to be and what they are), that resolve themselves in transcendent synthesis. Poems and even essays may operate according to a meditative logic—the speaker notices something, reflects on it, and arrives at a new understanding. Structurally, poems, like essays, often venture an initial assertion that the remainder of the work illustrates or proves. The body of John Logan's poem "Suzanne" affectionately illustrates or "proves" his opening thesis: "You make us want to stay alive, Suzanne."

Suzanne

You make us want to stay alive, Suzanne,
the way you turn

your blonde head,
The way you curve your slim hand

toward your breast.
When you drew your legs

up sitting by the fire,
and let your bronze hair

stream about your knees
I could see the grief

of the girl in your eyes.
It touched the high,

formal bones of your face.
Once I heard it in your lovely voice

when you sang—
the terrible time of being young.

Yet you bring us joy with your
self, Suzanne, wherever you are.

And once, although I wasn't here,
you left three roses on my stair.

One party night when you were high
you fled barefoot down the hall,

the fountain of your laughter
showering through the air.

"Chartreuse," you chanted
(the liqueur you always wanted),

"I have yellow chartreuse hair!"
Oh it was a great affair.

You were the most exciting person there.
Yesterday when I wasn't here

again,
you brought a blue, porcelain

egg to me—
colored beautifully

for the Russian Easter.
Since then, I have wanted to be your lover,

> but I have only touched your shoulder
> and let my fingers brush your hair,
>
> because you left three roses on my stair.

Once you have an inkling of the shape a draft is taking or might be made to assume, you're ready to trim the fat and build the muscle. Since it's generally easier to do the former than the latter, make sure you have a document ample enough to slim down. If you're afraid you don't, try writing more; write what might precede the first sentence or line and what might follow the last. Pick a point in the middle that seems less developed and open it up. Generally, be ruthless in what you toss and painstaking in your effort to fill in the blank spots.

How do you know what to cut? Remember the old elephant joke:

> How do you make an elephant out of a hunk of marble?
> Chip away anything that's not elephant.

Keep the "extras" (those incidental characters you could easily do without) for some future story in which they will star in a major role of their own. If characters stand stiffly in the background of your story or file past as shadowy members of the crowd, erase them and concentrate on the handful (even the one or two) essential to your tale. Try combining two characters into one: two partially developed siblings might merge into one fully developed character; two mean kids into one interesting bully. Consolidate your action. Sink your heels into one or two locations; don't jackrabbit from Kansas City to Krypton and on to Mission Control unless you're writing a novel, and even then you might want to reconsider such celestial gallivanting.

Paradoxically, when you shape a piece of writing, you both impose the most control and grant the work the most freedom freedom, in a sense, to dictate to you its final form, a form that may, in fact, differ from your original conception. In the introduction to Sylvia Plath's *Collected Poems*, poet Ted Hughes, her husband, acknowledges Plath's "artisan-like" adaptability:

> To my knowledge, she never scrapped any of her poetic efforts. With one or two exceptions, she brought every piece she worked on to some final form acceptable to her, rejecting at most the odd verse, or a false head, or a false tail. Her attitude to her verse was artisan-like: if she couldn't get a table out of the material, she was quite happy to get a chair, and even a toy.

In discovering your final form—be it table, chair, or toy—bear in mind the continuous interplay during revision between expansion and consolidation. Following intuition, taking risks, trying silly experiments, and creating excess should alternate with moments of evaluation in which you work to fuse the parts within the whole.

Beginnings

If you had asked me where I had begun the poem ["The Woman at the Washington Zoo"] I'd have said, "Why, Sir, at the beginning"; it was a surprise to me to see that I hadn't.

Randall Jarrell, *A Sad Heart at the Supermarket*

There is no need to begin at the "beginning" with the first words we set on a page. The actual beginnings give us a leg up, the boost needed to get on with the task, but they shouldn't be granted the place of privilege. Often these first words only vaguely mark our starting place; other times they point down a path we abandon when we get on our way. For the veteran writer, these first writings rarely find their way into final drafts as formal beginnings. In revision, they often become useless scaffolding no longer necessary to the final construction. In judging whether your story, essay, or poem has a strong beginning, ask yourself whether, if sitting in your dentist's waiting room and reading this initial paragraph or stanza, you would read past the first few lines. Recall your frustration when someone about to relate a joke, a piece of juicy gossip, or an important bit of news tells you too much background. Anxiously, you just want them to "get on with it."

The most compelling beginnings create immediate tension by referring to an array of "facts," meanwhile withholding the explanation that would make their connections clear. In other words, strong beginnings are often set *in medias res*, in the middle of things. It is as if writers assume in their readers a certain familiarity with the created world, which of course their readers don't have, and so must hurry up and read on in order to acquire it.

Consider the following openings:

I read about it in the paper, in the subway, on my way to work. I read it, and I couldn't believe it, and I read it again. Then perhaps I just stared at it, at the newsprint spelling out his name, spelling out the story. I stared at it in the swinging lights of the subway car, and in the faces and bodies of the people, and in my own face, trapped in the darkness that roared outside.

James Baldwin, "Sonny's Blues"

At four o'clock
in the gun-metal blue dark
we hear the first crow of the first cock

just below
the gun-metal blue window
and immediately there is an echo

Elizabeth Bishop, "Roosters"

The secret to diving under a moving freight train and rolling out the other side with all your parts attached lies in picking the right spot between the tracks to hit with your back. Ideally, you want soft dirt or pea gravel, clear of glass shards and railroad spikes that could cause you instinctively, and fatally, to sit up. Today, at thirty-eight, I couldn't be threatened or baited enough to attempt that dive. But as a seventh grader struggling to make the cut in a tough Atlanta grammar school, all it took was a dare.

Roger Hoffman, "The Dare"

Striking about each of these examples is the number of "moves" the author executes at once: establishing point of view, voice or persona, and a sense of time; offering concrete images; and in the case of the poem, establishing phrasing. Consider the direction in which each provokes the reader. One can't read the beginning of Baldwin's story without asking, "Who is the *he?*" What is his relation to the *I*, and what is the *it* that so preoccupies the speaker? Even in the first few sentences, we want to solve the puzzle of the relationship between the speaker and the subject of the newspaper article.

Baldwin piques our curiosity, while Bishop tunes our ears in her artfully simple opening. She begins her poem with a single rooster's crow calling forth the crow of another rooster, and in repetition establishes the pattern of reverberation that will echo through the entire poem. Notice the "gun-metal blue dark" and the "gun-metal blue window." Read the lines aloud, and hear the "k" sound at the end of each line in the first stanza and the "o" at the end of each line in the second, the two sounds that, in fact, make up the rooster's call.

Hoffman begins his essay ironically in the voice of standard process analysis, but like the others he opens with a burst of energy, creating a dense, convincing world. These writers inundate their readers with information, some stated, but most implied, and force the audience to read on to see how it all fits together.

EXERCISE: Opening Lines

Look back through your notebook or through any rough drafts you are currently working on, and find at least five provocative sentences or lines: for example, "We could shoot baskets after hours anytime we wanted back then, because David was still alive."

Type each of these onto a blank sheet of paper, along with any other treasures that precede or follow it. Imagine these as the opening lines of your first paragraph or stanza. Ask yourself: Who is the implied speaker? What images or scenes does this opening inspire? What would I have to do to deliver on their promises?

Choose one, and outline how the prose or poetry might follow from this forceful beginning.

•   •   •

Notice that the lively sentences or lines you find buried in drafts or jottings are almost never at the start of a piece of writing; they emerge from the creative ooze once you have warmed up. Whatever gets you to them (some exercise in this book perhaps) is useful and necessary, but it's important to recognize the superfluity of the preliminary writing once you begin to discern your final goal, however blurred, and be ready to cut that excess away.

The following opening by a student vaguely introduces character and context in the first two paragraphs, but consider what a stronger beginning actually presents itself in the third paragraph ("His uncle had been the one to introduce him to agates"). Once this promise of semi-precious stones has hooked the reader, the more predictable description of beach and ocean can be condensed and subordinated to the story's main action as it unfolds.

> The boy never considered that he may not be the only person in the world who was awake so early. To him, stepping on the cool, sifting sand at first light made him the first person on Earth to see the day. The beach, with all its driftwood, and the bordering ocean were so vast that it was easy to forget other places in the world, and that they even existed. It excited Ben to have such a large, beautiful beach all to himself. With sleep still in his eyes, he walked on towards the increasing roar of the breaking surf. He loved the sound. In fact, he had been able to faintly hear the ocean from the campground, where his family was still asleep, almost half a mile away.
>
> His sandals made a constant clap as they slapped the bottoms of his feet. The soft, gray sand would partially bury the sandals every step he took, making it seem to take forever to reach the water's edge. Ben didn't mind, though, for he was preoccupied with studying

the vast beach for patches of newly washed up rocks. Although only eight years old, Ben had spent over half of the summers in his life on this beach. And he knew, as well as anyone, the best places the tide liked to leave its treasures.

His uncle had been the one to introduce him to agates. Ben didn't remember which summer it was, but he could remember the excitement he felt when his uncle picked up a rock, held it to the sky, and let the sun's light make the agate glow with warmth and color. His uncle explained how some wonderful magic on the bottom of the ocean floor had made these see-through rocks. Usually agates weren't much bigger than a match-box car. But once or twice every summer Ben would come upon an agate the size of a small pear!

Corey Stapleton

Middles

Opening paragraphs and lines will come to you as you're walking along, and of course suitable general subjects occur to you all the time ("that would make an interesting story"; "I ought to try a poem about that"), but getting through the middle can erode the faith and confidence of the most committed writer.

The creative process typically moves through a manic-depressive cycle with bursts of imaginative energy so exuberant you can't seem to write fast enough, followed by bouts of malaise when your words appear stillborn on the page. When in the middle of completing a work you sink into one of these periods of inactivity, you've encountered a typically invisible barrier—invisible because if you could identify the problem, chances are you could fix it, and in time get on toward the end. Sometimes if you step aside for a moment, the obstruction will disappear and you'll be able to proceed to the end.

Let the following serve as productive diversions:

1. Write a letter to a character, speaker, or subject in your work in progress (story, poem, or essay).
2. Place a character in a setting alien to your story (in a gym class, on *Oprah Winfrey*, at church).
3. Imagine a character is sitting right there beside you as you compose, and write down his or her complaints about the story.
4. Tell about something happening in your story from the point of view of a minor character.
5. If you're stalled in your work on a poem, print it out with large spaces between each line. Cut the poem into strips, one for each

line, and rearrange them. You'll immediately spot your weakest lines. Toss them out and work on the transitions between the strong lines.

6. Change the tense of every verb. If you've written in past tense, change each verb to present.

7. If you're working on a personal essay, begin your essay with the last paragraph you wrote.

8. If your story, poem, or essay is about a person, stop and describe that person's gestures (when he or she is angry, sad, excited, and so on).

9. Hunt for the "oh too perfect" or the "all too vile" character, setting, mood, or thought, and add a tincture of the opposite. Give your dazzling blonde a bad habit and your suicidal freshman a small moment of humor or joy. After all, there *are* ants in the sand, and even criminals love their mothers!

10. Play devil's advocate and show that the major thrust of your essay is all wrong.

These simple practices, though they may yield no fresh passages for the final product, will nevertheless help you think in a new way about the work in progress. Just as you need tension to get you started, you need it to recharge your writing somewhere in the middle. Looking back over what you have written so far, what new possibilities might you consider introducing in order to energize an uninspiring character, action, image, or idea? Notebook Options in preceding chapters may offer further refreshing suggestions.

Endings

Last lines are like first lines; they often just come like gifts. Ideally, they close the piece without nailing down every issue. Too often student endings are too final: someone is killed off; the speaker awakens, making everything that passed before a dream; a last line hammers home the meaning of the poem. Last lines require a mixture of closure and openness, a combination of delicacy and boldness. William Butler Yeats ends many of his poems with questions. Look at the ending of James Wright's poem "In Ohio":

> White mares lashed to the sulky carriages
> Trot softly
> Around the dismantled fairgrounds
> Near Buckeye Lake.

The sandstone blocks of a wellspring
Cool dark green moss.

The sun floats down, a small golden lemon dissolves
In the water.

I dream, as I lean over the edge, of a crawdad's mouth.

The cellars of haunted houses are like ancient cities,
Fallen behind a big heap of apples.

A widow on a front porch puckers her lips
And whispers.

The hollow "o" sounds of *Ohio* resonate in the circle of horses racing around the fairgrounds, in a well, in the reflected sun, in a crawdad's mouth, in cellars, and finally in the "o" on the whispering lips of the widow.

Last lines often present themselves, but the process of editing and refining never ends. Works of writing only approach perfection; they never actually reach it.

Chapter 11

The Poem

I asked a poet friend one time what it was that poets did, and he thought awhile, and then he told me, "They extend the language."

Kurt Vonnegut

What is a poem? For hundreds of years, writers have debated this question, defending contradictory definitions that, on the whole, reveal more about the values of individual writers and the attitudes of the society in which they live than about the absolute qualities of poetry. Some writers characterize the poem as a highly crafted object, a vessel into which the poet pours sentiments, ideas, and observations; others understand form and meaning as inextricably entwined. Still others see poetry as mystical revelation cast down from some benevolent deity, thrust forward from one's unconscious, or percolating up from a collective unconscious we all share. For many modern writers, poetry thrives on the personal, but for T. S. Eliot, poetry stands at a consciously crafted distance: "It is not the expression of personality, but an escape from personality." Yet, reacting against the overintellectualizing of poetic interpretation, Archibald MacLeish protests in "Ars Poetica":

> A poem should not mean
> But be.

For William Carlos Williams, a poem is simply "energy" transferred from the poet, via the poem, to the reader.

Some poets intend their poems as manifestos; others as intimate secrets, as subtle whispers, or as clenched fists. Some employ the most esoteric of references; others the commonest. Poems, like other forms of writing (both fictive and nonfictive), are written for a variety of purposes and produce a broad range of responses. Only the naïve reader demands

120

that poems be of only one sort and produce only a narrow range of emotion. When we abandon our expectations about what a poem *should be*, we discover that some poems soothe, while others unnerve, excite, or merely amuse. We nod in silent acknowledgment at certain poems, luxuriate in the lush language of others, or find ourselves haunted by a poem or a single line days, even years, after we've read it.

Although rationalist formal education prepares us to understand by first establishing categories (the sonnet is this, the ballad that; the haiku is this, the epic that), the rich variety of poetry, both contemporary and ancient, belies simple definition. Poems, like novels or plays, obey no absolute rules and serve no single purpose; rather they adapt to the distinct needs of specific times and of individual poets who find themselves compelled for personal, emotional, political, and in certain cases even economic, motives to make an endless variety of statements in crafted language. Trying to settle on a definition of poetry or on any absolute sense of the effect poems produce in readers is often counterproductive to writing poems. Any definition we formulate precludes others and imprisons us prematurely in a partial understanding of poetry.

Other cultures contribute even more variety to the term *poetry*. In many third-world nations, poetry enjoys a greater place of importance among the general population than it does in the United States. In the West African country of Ghana, for example, young poets frequently read their poems at public gatherings. Daniel Ortega, the leader of Sandinista-ruled Nicaragua and himself a poet, once said, "In Nicaragua everybody is considered to be a poet until he proves to the contrary."

Just as poetry appears in an endless variety of styles—from casual and sassy in one instance to fitting and proper in another—so also does its subject range widely. Although more lines of poetry have been written about love and death than about any other subjects, consider the assortment of poetic subjects limitless, and bear in mind that it is probably much easier to write an interesting poem about your baseball cap than it is to write one about your broken heart. With the latter comes an emotion so immediate and overwhelming it insists on profundity. But conscious efforts to be profound typically end in failure; all too often the poems constructed to support such burdens fall apart under their weight.

Making Use of Familiar Forms

If it's finally impossible to say that poems are written in a certain way, about a certain group of subjects, to satisfy a certain set of needs on behalf of their readers, then what generalizations are left to make about poetry? William Stafford suggests a radical notion: that poetry, in both the reader and the writer, calls forth a way of perceiving language that will "make something not a poem become a poem by looking at it a certain way, or listening to it a certain way."

The Found Poem

The *found poem* may be a matchbook ad, a news item, or an administrative memo taken out of context, with sentences and sometimes even individual words fragmented in provocative ways—"something not a poem" that has "become a poem by looking at it in a certain way." In the found poem, the poet "extends the language" in Vonnegut's terms and quite often satirically comments on the original. Notice the obvious linguistic playfulness in this student's found poem based on a professor's introductory comments from an engineering course syllabus:

To the Stud

ent: You are a
bout to ex (a)
mine material
that will cap
tivate
and en
gross you.
Take time
to gr
asp the id
eas and con
cepts.
Make a D
et er
mine D
eFFort.
After all the class
revolves around
just three
fun
dam
mentals:

energy,
entropy,
and proper
ties.

Brett Howe

The audience for this class assignment, uniformed midshipmen at the Naval Academy, particularly enjoyed the humor of this poem for they, too, had endured the hardships of this unpopular required course, all the while attending to shined shoes and "proper ties."

EXERCISE: The Found Poem

Look through ads, travel brochures, textbooks, the daily paper, and tabloids for a short passage (a few sentences) that might be interpreted in more than one way or that has a few interesting words you might play with. Experiment with line breaks, noticing that as you break a piece of prose into lines you create emphasis, with the greatest emphasis resting automatically on the word at the end of a line.

The List

Many of the exercises in this book ask you to make a *list* as a way of warming up, a way of clearing your mind of the "tip-of-the-tongue" first and usually predictable choices in order to uncover the more interesting third and fourth possibilities. But the list is a legitimate poetic form in itself. From its ancient roots as litany or prayer, through its American variants in the poems of Walt Whitman to Allen Ginsberg, the list invokes the infinite through its encyclopedic inclusion of example after example. But the poetic list is not a simple disorganized collection; it is a movement and progression. In the following excerpt from the poem "Faces," Whitman moves from the abstract ("Faces of friendship, caution, and fear"), to the generic (faces of hunters, fishers, artist, and infants), and, finally, to the particular (the face of a quaker woman framed by her quaker hat and her cream-hued gown made for her by her grandchildren):

Sauntering the pavement or riding the country by-road,
    such faces!
Faces of the singing of music, the grand faces of natural
    lawyers and judges broad at the back-top,

The faces of hunters and fishers bulged at the brows, the
 shaved blanch'd faces of orthodox citizens,
The pure, extravagant, yearning, questioning artist's face,
The sacred faces of infants, the illuminated face of the
 mother of many children,
The face as of a dream, the face of an immobile rock,
The wild hawk, his wings clipp'd by the slipper,

Behold a woman!
She looks out from her quaker cap, her face is clearer and
 more beautiful than the sky.
She sits in an armchair under the shaded porch of the
 farmhouse,
The sun just shines on her old white head.
Her ample gown is of cream-hued linen.
Her grandsons raised the flax, and her granddaughters spun
 it with the distaff and the wheel.

The incantatory effect of the list poem can serve the poet as manifesto. In the following poem, Lawrence Ferlinghetti ranges widely with comments on American commercialism, popular culture, sexuality, racism, as well as Western literature:

I Am Waiting

I am waiting for my case to come up
and I am waiting
for a rebirth of wonder
and I am waiting for someone
to really discover America and wail
and I am waiting
for the discovery
of a new symbolic western frontier
and I am waiting
for the American Eagle
to really spread its wings
and straighten up and fly right
and I am waiting
for the Age of Anxiety
to drop dead
and I am waiting
for the war to be fought
which will make the world safe

for anarchy
and I am waiting
for the final withering away
of all governments
and I am perpetually awaiting
a rebirth of wonder

I am waiting for the Second Coming
and I am waiting
for a religious revival
to sweep thru the state of Arizona
and I am waiting
for the Grapes of Wrath to be stored
and I am waiting
for them to prove
that God is really American
and I am seriously waiting
for Billy Graham and Elvis Presley
to exchange roles seriously
and I am waiting
to see God on television
piped onto church altars
if only they can find
the right channel
to tune in on
and I am waiting
for the Last Supper to be served again
with a strange new appetizer
and I am perpetually awaiting
a rebirth of wonder

I am waiting for my number to be called
and I am waiting
for the living end
and I am waiting
for dad to come home
his pockets full
of irradiated silver dollars
and I am waiting
for the atomic tests to end
and I am waiting happily
for things to get much worse
before they improve

and I am waiting for the Salvation Army to take over
and I am waiting
for the human crowd
to wander off a cliff somewhere
clutching its atomic umbrella
and I am waiting
for Ike to act
and I am waiting
for the meek to be blessed
and inherit the earth
without taxes
and I am waiting
for forests and animals
to reclaim the earth as theirs
and I am waiting
for a way to be devised
to destroy all nationalisms
without killing anybody
and I am waiting
for linnets and planets to fall like rain
and I am waiting for lovers and weepers
to lie down together again
in a new rebirth of wonder

I am waiting for the Great Divide to be crossed
and I am anxiously waiting
for the secret of eternal life to be discovered
by an obscure general practitioner
and save me forever from certain death
and I am waiting
for life to begin
and I am waiting
for the storms of life
to be over
and I am waiting
to set sail for happiness
and I am waiting
for a reconstructed Mayflower
to reach America
with its picture story and tv rights
sold in advance to the natives
and I am waiting

for the lost music to sound again
in the Lost Continent
in a new rebirth of wonder

I am waiting for the day
that maketh all things clear
and I am waiting
for Ole Man River
to just stop rolling along
past the country club
and I am waiting
for the deepest South
to just stop Reconstructing itself
in its own image
and I am waiting
for a sweet desegregated chariot
to swing low
and carry me back to Ole Virginie
and I am waiting
for Ole Virginie to discover
just why Darkies are born
and I am waiting
for God to lookout
from Lookout Mountain
and see the *Ode to the Confederate Dead*
as a real farce
and I am awaiting retribution
for what America did
to Tom Sawyer
and I am perpetually awaiting
a rebirth of wonder

I am waiting for Tom Swift to grow up
and I am waiting
for the American Boy
to take off Beauty's clothes
and get on top of her
and I am waiting
for Alice in Wonderland
to retransmit to me
her total dream of innocence
and I am waiting
for Childe Roland to come

to the final darkest tower
and I am waiting
for Aphrodite
to grow live arms
at a final disarmament conference
in a new rebirth of wonder

I am waiting
to get some intimations
of immortality
by recollecting my early childhood
and I am waiting
for the green mornings to come again
youth's dumb green fields come back again
and I am waiting
for some strains of unpremeditated art
to shake my typewriter
and I am waiting to write
the great indelible poem
and I am waiting
for the last long careless rapture
and I am perpetually waiting
for the fleeing lovers on the Grecian Urn
to catch each other up at last
and embrace
and I am waiting
perpetually and forever
a renaissance of wonder

EXERCISE: The List Poem

Select one of the following openings (or invent one of your own), and write a list of at least thirty sentences, each beginning with the same opening clause. Let the subjects of your sentences range widely—from the personal to the public, from the casual to the profound.

I have known (or I know, We know, You know, They know)
I have seen (or I see)
I am listening to (or for)
Let there be
We have bought (or We will buy)
We have desired (or I desire, We desire)

Avoid an endless series of short sentences ("I know physics. I know math. I know chemistry."), and vary their content to allow for striking juxtaposition. When you've written at least thirty, group them in an interesting order, adding and subtracting as you wish, and title your list poem.

Posing Questions

Although modern poets like Robert Lowell and John Berryman have found great comfort in the sonnet's "narrow room," most contemporary poets prefer a more open form. Some even make striking use of common rhetorical forms, everyday forms that we don't typically regard as "poetic." For example, Denise Levertov employs the *question-and-answer* form in the following poem to protest the Vietnam War, a tragedy, according to Levertov, that resulted in a brutal assault on the Vietnamese people. Levertov's melancholic poem groups the questions into one stanza and the answers into another, and enlivens them with startling insight.

What Were They Like?

1) Did the people of Vietnam
   use lanterns of stone?
2) Did they hold ceremonies
   to reverence the opening of buds?
3) Were they inclined to quiet laughter?
4) Did they use bone and ivory,
   jade and silver, for ornament?
5) Had they an epic poem?
6) Did they distinguish between speech and singing?

1) Sir, their light hearts turned to stone
   It is not remembered whether in gardens
   stone lanterns illumined pleasant ways.
2) Perhaps they gathered once to delight in blossom,
   but after the children were killed
   there were no more buds.
3) Sir, laughter is bitter to the burned mouth.
4) A dream ago, perhaps. Ornament is for joy.
   All the bones were charred.
5) It is not remembered. Remember,
   most were peasants; their life
   was in rice and bamboo.

When peaceful clouds were reflected in the paddies
and the water buffalo stepped surely along terraces,
maybe fathers told their sons old tales.
When bombs smashed those mirrors
there was time only to scream.
6) There is an echo yet
of their speech which was like a song.
It was reported their singing resembled the flight
of moths in moonlight.
Who can say? It is silent now.

The first half of this poem posits an extinct culture, asking about its artifacts, its literature, and its ceremonies. The second half, ironically echoing the language of the first half (of light, growth, speech, and song), establishes the contrast between the simple, lively agrarian life of the past and the still, silent death of a culture brought about by war, a war that turned hearts to stone, prohibited generation, and replaced tales with screams. Only the final image of the moths in moonlight resurrects the culture that war has attempted to obliterate.

EXERCISE: The Question-and-Answer Poem

Select a topic about which you have strong feelings. Write a series of questions and answers relating to the topic that reveal subtly and through your choice of particular words a passion for the subject. Resist the impulse to turn this into a funny poem. Try to write about a topic you take seriously in order to make people think twice.

The Letter

Another familiar literary form that all of us have practiced since childhood is the *letter*—letters of complaint, of thanks, of friendship, and of anger. To a sister or brother, we may have written curt notes taped to our bedroom doors, maybe something as simple and unambiguous as "Stay Out or Else!" To a distant lover or to a friendly confidant we may have disclosed in a letter things hidden from others. In the intensity of resentment or love or loneliness, we've written (or at least imagined) letters we never sent. While reading the following poems, imagine the intended audience of each letter poem, and note the amazing variety available through this form.

Inviting a Friend to Supper

Tonight, grave sir, both my poor house, and I
Do equally desire your company;
Not that we think us worthy such a guest,
But that your worth will dignify our feast
With those that come, whose grace may make that seem
Something, which else could hope for no esteem.
It is the fair acceptance, sir, creates
The entertainment perfect, not the cates.
Yet shall you have, to rectify your palate,
An olive, capers, or some better salad
Ushering the mutton; with a short-legged hen,
If we can get her, full of eggs, and then
Lemons, and wine for sauce; to these a coney
Is not to be despaired of, for our money;
And, though fowl now be scarce, yet there are clerks,
The sky not falling, think we may have larks.
I'll tell you of more, and lie so you will come:
Of partridge, pheasant, woodcock, of which some
May yet be there, and godwit, if we can;
Knot, rail, and ruff too. Howsoe'er, my man
Shall read a piece of Virgil, Tacitus,
Livy, or of some better book to us.
Of which we'll speak our minds, amidst our meat;
And I'll profess no verses to repeat.
To this, if aught appear which I not know of,
That will the pastry, not my paper, show off.
Digestive cheese and fruit there sure will be;
But that which most doth take my Muse and me,
Is a pure cup of rich Canary wine,
Which is the Mermaid's now, but shall be mine;
Of which had Horace, or Anacreon tasted,
Their lives, as do their lines, till now had lasted.
Tobacco, nectar, or the Thespian spring,
Are all but Luther's beer to this I sing.
Of this we will sup free, but moderately,
And we will have no Pooley, or Parrot by,
Nor shall our cups make any guilty men;
But, at our parting we will be as when
We innocently met. No simple word
That shall be uttered at our mirthful board,

Shall make us sad next morning of affright
The liberty that we'll enjoy tonight.

Ben Jonson

Letter

I have wanted to begin
by telling you I saw another
tanager below the pond
where I had sat for half an hour
feeding on wild berries
in the little clearing near the pines
that hide the lower field
and then looked up from red berries
to the quick red bird brilliant
in the light. I have seen
more yarrow and swaying
Queen Anne's lace around the woods
as hawkweed and nightshade
wither and drop seed. A new blue flower,
sweet, yellow-stamened, ovary inferior,
has recently sprung up.
                    But I had the odd
feeling, walking to the house
to write this down, that I had left
the birds and flowers in the field,
rooted or feeding. They are not in my head,
are not now on this page.
It was very strange to me, but I think
their loss was your absence. I wanted
to be walking up with Leif, the sun
behind us skipping off the pond,
the windy maple sheltering the house,
and find you there and say
here! a new blue flower (ovary inferior)
and busy Leif and Kris with naming
in a world I love. You even have
my field guide. It's you I love.
I have believed so long
in the magic of names and poems.
I hadn't thought them bodiless
at all. Tall Buttercup. Wild Vetch.

"Often I am permitted to return
to a meadow." It all seemed real to me
last week. Words. You are the body
of my world, root and flower, the
brightness and surprise of birds.
I miss you, love. Tell Leif
you're the names of things.

Robert Haas

EXERCISE: The Letter Poem

The authors of the preceding poems make use of sensory detail (hyperbolic detail in the Jonson poem) to communicate with the invited guest and a loved one. For another example, turn back to Chapter 9: Choosing a Point of View, to William Carlos Williams's "This Is Just to Say," which is written in the form of a note to a person who got to the refrigerator too late to have the last juicy plum.

Write a letter to someone you know or to someone from your past in which you describe a certain scene, event, or incident in sensory detail.

Trim the excess and transform this letter into a poem.

Traditional Poetic Form: The Sestina

Experiments with conventional forms may not yield a satisfying finished product, but they may stretch you beyond what you thought you wanted or meant to say. And, like musical études, they will always increase your nimbleness with language. In many creative writing classes, exercises dedicated to fixed forms tend to feature such intricacies as the sonnet, the ode, and the ballad. Unfortunately, these exercises often result in the "mathematically" correct form, decorated on the outside but hollow on the inside. One of the simplest conventional forms and a good starting place is the *sestina*, a verse form with six unrhymed sestets (six-line stanzas), each with the same set of final words arranged in different order. The sestina concludes with a three-line stanza that incorporates all six repeated words. Modern poets Ezra Pound and W. H. Auden and contemporary poets Donald Justice and W. D. Snodgrass have displayed the virtues of the sestina. In her beautifully provocative "Sestina," Elizabeth Bishop demonstrates through a series of echoes the power of the form to bring together in clear resonance the six end words: *house, grandmother, child, stove, almanac,* and *tears*:

Sestina

September rain falls on the house.
In the failing light, the old grandmother
sits in the kitchen with the child
beside the Little Marvel Stove,
reading the jokes from the almanac,
laughing and talking to hide her tears.

She thinks that her equinoctial tears
and the rain that beats on the roof of the house
were both foretold by the almanac,
but only known to a grandmother.
The iron kettle sings on the stove.
She cuts some bread and says to the child,

It's time for tea now; but the child
is watching the teakettle's small hard tears
dance like mad on the hot black stove,
the way the rain must dance on the house.
Tidying up, the old grandmother
hangs up the clever almanac

on its string. Birdlike, the almanac
hovers half open above the child,
hovers above the old grandmother
and her teacup full of dark brown tears.
She shivers and says she thinks the house
feels chilly, and puts more wood in the stove.

It was to be, says the Marvel Stove.
I know what I know, says the almanac.
With crayons the child draws a rigid house
and a winding pathway. Then the child
puts in a man with buttons like tears
and shows it proudly to the grandmother.

But secretly, while the grandmother
busies herself about the stove,
the little moons fall down like tears
from between the pages of the almanac
into the flower bed the child
has carefully placed in the front of the house.

Time to plant tears, says the almanac.
The grandmother sings to the marvellous stove
and the child draws another inscrutable house.

In a more lyrical, less narrative version of the sestina, Nancy P. Arbuthnot takes a few more liberties with the form and drops the final three-line
stanza:

Late Spring

Long shadows on the grass: late
afternoon. The slanted light leaves
the hills a paler
green. Carrying a vase plumed
with iris and peony, half-hidden, you appear,
eyes too blue

insects crawling the stems. Blue
afternoon. It is later
than it appears:
behind the jewelled leaves
you are tired. The plumes
of the iris, the pale

peonies bob, impaled
on their stems. A steel-blue
moth flutters the plumes.
It has grown so late!
Still, you've come, with leaves
you peer

through, the moth whispers
in. I take the flowers—pale
flames. Across the drop-leaf
you are silent. I talk of horses, blue
whales that heave the sky. Later
the whales breach, spout plume

on flaming plume—
or so it appears
as the clouds catch the late
light, then pale.
So afternoon fades. Your blue
eyes darken. You say you'll leave

but finger the leaves,
the torch-plumes
or iris. Somewhere far off *Blue*
Bayou plays. You disappear.
The stars pale.
It's late.

EXERCISE: The Sestina

Have a go at a sestina yourself. Either write six 6-line stanzas in which you end your lines with the same set of six words (just mixing them up), or follow more closely the formal model, which presents end words in the following order:

1st stanza: 1,2,3,4,5,6
2nd stanza: 6,1,5,2,4,3
3rd stanza: 3,6,4,1,2,5
4th stanza: 5,3,2,6,1,4
5th stanza: 4,5,1,3,6,2
6th stanza: 2,4,6,5,3,1

Write a final three-line stanza with one of the core words in the middle of each line and another at the end. Often after the second or third stanza of the sestina, you'll be forced into wild improvising in order to keep the cycle going, but it is precisely the result of this pushing and stretching that will sometimes produce the most interesting lines.

•   •   •

A note of caution: you can produce a mathematically perfect English sonnet, for example, with strict rhyme scheme (*abab cdcd efef gg*) that lies dead and empty on the page. Even perfect form will not rescue dull language. When you have to choose between strict adherence to form and powerful language, elect the latter, for without it you'll have an empty shell, not a poem.

Seeing, As If for the First Time

As contemporary poetry becomes smaller, less aural (more writerly), and more preoccupied with the moment, the particular, and the personal than with the universal, it calls for the reader to pause in a world that repudiates pause, to notice language in a world where words wash over us in a daily babble, and to see the common and the ordinary in all its particular beauty. Poetry, by means of its lines, invites us to see something, however simple, as if for the first time:

Between Walls

the wings
of the

hospital where
nothing

will grow lie
cinders

in which shine
the broken

pieces of a green
bottle

William Carlos Williams

Like so many of Williams's poems, "Between Walls" delicately calls our attention to something simple by violating the typical way in which we group words into clauses. The line breaks separate adjectives from the nouns they modify ("broken / pieces"; "green / bottle") and join the ends of clauses with the beginnings of others ("hospital where"; "will grow lie") to call our attention to the meaning of simple things, objects that compose a picture of the outside of the hospital, one that comments on the hospital's interior. Had Williams written *bank* instead of *hospital*, the poem would have been a different poem entirely.

EXERCISE: Interior Poem

Note the ways in which the following Williams poem captures in concrete but evocative detail a simple interior scene.

Nantucket

Flowers through the window
lavender and yellow

changed by white curtains—
Smell of cleanliness—

> Sunshine of late afternoon—
> On the glass tray
>
> a glass pitcher, the tumbler
> turned down, by which
>
> a key is lying—And the
> immaculate white bed

Now envision yourself opening a door either in memory or imagination and beholding a room. Allow your eyes to survey the room along the same path that Williams's followed as he took in the room in Nantucket, from the window to the view outside, to the smell inside, to certain prominent furnishings. Then write a poem incorporating the details of the interior you see. If you wish, you might also try to arrange your details into a similar formal pattern, five two-line stanzas with four to seven syllables per line, and invent a title.

The Line

In his sixteenth-century poem "The Tunning of Elinour Rumming," about an ugly, disreputable woman, John Skelton uses short lines to create a humorous description of this bawdy alcoholic character:

> Droopy and drowsy,
> Scurvy and lousy;
> Her face all bowsy,
> Comely crinkled,
> Wondersly wrinkled,
> Like a roast pig's ear,
> Bristled with hear.
>   Her lewd lips twain.
> They slaver, men sain,
> Like a ropy rain,
> A gummy glair.
> she is ugly fair . . .

A contemporary of Skelton, Edward de Vere, Earl of Oxford, bemoans an assault made on his good name in his poem "His Good Name Being Blemished" with lines three times as long as Skelton's:

> Help gods, help saints, help sprites and powers that in the
>   heaven do dwell!

> Help ye that are to wail ay wont, ye howling hounds of
>   hell!
> Help man, help beasts, help birds and worms that on the
>   earth doth toil!
> Help fish, help fowl that flocks and feeds upon the salt sea
>   soil!
> Help echo this in air doth flee, shrill voices to resound,
> To wail this loss of my good name, as of these griefs the
>   ground.

As these two examples illustrate, poets have always employed varying line lengths. But contemporary poets have taken line length to its logical extreme (the one-word line, on the one hand, the long line that wraps around from margin to margin, on the other). The following passage from Dave Smith's "Boats" illustrates the undulating long line and underscores the speaker's lament over the inevitable replacement of one way of life, complete with "cunners" (boats that ferry out to oyster scows), with another.

> When the dozers come to take the marsh, slapping down layers of asphalt, when the all-temperature malls rise, when women of the garden club cease their designing, cunners will be gone, claimed by antique freaks, smashed for scrap, the creeks leveled, the sun deceived with only absence flashing in the heat.

What happens to the passage if you break it up into short lines?

Poets Robert Creeley and David Ignatow employ a shorter line suited to the development of analogies:

The Flower

> I think I grow tensions
> like flowers
> in a wood where
> nobody goes.
>
> Every wound is perfect,
> encloses itself in a tiny
> imperceptible blossom,
> making pain.
>
> Pain is a flower like that one,
> like this one,
> like that one,
> like this one.
>
> > Robert Creeley

And the Same Words

I like rust on a nail,
fog on a mountain.
Clouds hide stars,
rooms have doors,
eyes close,
and the same words
that began love
end it
with changed emphasis.

David Ignatow

Consider the prevalence of the sentence in the poem. Structurally, Smith's stanza is one sentence, Creeley's poem, three sentences. And Ignatow's? Poetry, like music, requires a sense of phrasing, of periodic openings and closings. The best way to learn to sense such phrasing is to read profusely—not just the five or six poems of a given writer anthologized in a particular collection, but the fifty poems that poet has gathered into a book. Note the tightly impacted poetic sentence with modifying clause after modifying clause versus the simple comparison broken into three or four lines. No matter how syntactically convoluted they appear, no matter how fragmented they read, most poems employ the essential elements of a sentence—subject and predicate. The novice poet, diligently accumulating adjectives and nouns, often omits the engine that drives it all—the strong verb.

The more you read poetry, the keener sense you will develop for the elasticity of language. From simile to metaphor, Creeley's poem creates the tension of bringing together two dissimilar things—pain and a flower—and delicately establishes a resonance between them. In Ignatow's poem, the line "end it" carries the most weight; the final line supplements its meaning, forcing us to consider the way in which we might read each of the images before us in a slightly altered way (the rust covering a nail versus the nail covered by rust, clouds that hide stars versus the stars hidden by clouds, doors that open and doors that close, and so on.

EXERCISE: Line Breaks

Locate either a descriptive passage of prose from your notebook or a poem you're working on, and experiment with line breaks. Try writing the same passage or poem three different ways: with long rhythmic lines, with short, two-to-four-word lines, and with a pattern of alternating short and long lines. Such experimentation will reveal words that you can do without as well as holes that need filling. Trim and supplement where you sense the need.

Revisionary Mythmaking

Poets revive dull words and dead phrases, and they invigorate the models they inherit from preceding generations. Some feminist poets, in particular, have set on the path of revisionary mythmaking, rewriting in contemporary contexts the biblical stories and fairy tales told to us as children. Anne Sexton's *Transformations*, for example, reinvents the fairy tales "Snow White," "Rumpelstiltskin," "Rapunzel," "Little Red Riding Hood," "Hansel and Gretel," and others in a collection of sometimes bitter, sometimes funny poems. For example, she introduces the poem "Cinderella" with contemporary versions of the rags-to-riches motif:

> You always read about it:
> the plumber with twelve children
> who wins the Irish Sweepstakes.
> From toilets to riches.
> That story.
>
> Or the nursemaid,
> some luscious sweet from Denmark
> who captures the oldest son's heart.
> From diapers to Dior.
> That story.
>
> Or the milkman who serves the wealthy,
> eggs, cream, butter, yogurt, milk,
> the white truck like an ambulance
> who goes into real estate
> and makes a pile.
> From homogenized to martinis at lunch.
>
> Or the charwoman
> who is on the bus when it cracks up
> and collects enough from the insurance.
> From mops to Bonwit Teller.
> That story.

Once
the wife of a rich man was on her deathbed
and she said to her daughter Cinderella:
Be devout. Be good. Then I will smile
down from heaven in the seam of a cloud . . .

EXERCISE: A Modern Myth

Select a fairy tale, a religious story, an historical event, a popular legend, or even a commercial, and retell it from a different point of view. For example, speak as the wolf in "Little Red Riding Hood," as a Panamanian child watching American paratroopers fall from the sky in her neighborhood in Panama City, or as the parent of the ultrathin, slinky model in a sexy ad.

Revising

The process of writing poetry is filled with fits and starts; therefore, this chapter more than any other in this section of the book contains an abundance of exercises. The virtue of the poem is its size; if one effort to get going isn't successful, you can always idle for a moment and try again. Writing a poem, according to William Stafford, is like starting a car on ice.

But once your poem is on a roll, and you're ready to revise, put into practice a fierce economy, an economy in which every word counts. Search out and eliminate the vague, slippery words. Instead of "The woods seemed to wail that cold November night," substitute "The woods wailed that cold November night," or recast the poem in the present tense. Sometimes, simply changing from past to present tense can enliven a poem in exciting ways. Be alert to *-ing* words that often make their lazy way into the first draft of a poem. By transforming these into active verbs, you replace the vague timelessness that *-ing* words suggest with immediacy and force.

Consider the following two lines of the first draft of a poem:

Some ideas dance through my mind
Waltzing with freedom.

More precise than *dance*, *waltz* would be a better verb for the first line. In addition to eliminating *-ing* words (*shimmering* and *cascading* are particular culprits in first drafts), the writer needs to ask a number of questions aimed at focusing other areas of imprecision: What ideas are "some ideas"? What does it mean to waltz "with freedom"? Does the image border on cliché ("visions of sugar plums danced through their heads")? By demanding that each word speak more precisely, the writer ultimately achieves a clearer meaning; the sharp and crystalline replace the misty and formless.

The following writer achieves increased precision by eliminating -*ing* words from a first draft of a stanza of a poem about a pine lizard:

First draft:

> Reflecting sunlight from black eyes
> his face is ancient.
> Blue belly heaving
> against dry bark
> he is holding on.

Second draft:

> Ancient black eyes
> reflect the sunlight.
> A blue belly heaves
> against dry bark,
> as delicate feet hold fast.

In the second draft, the writer eliminates all forms of the verb *be*, gives nouns agency ("eyes reflect," "a blue belly heaves," and "feet hold"), and concentrates attention on the lizard's eyes rather than on its nondescript face.

As you tighten the lines of your own poems, work toward efficiency, and make each word work overtime for you, don't forget, that in doing so you may expose a few holes. Revision is not only a process of elimination; it often requires expansion as well as contraction (see Chapter 10: Shaping for a more complete discussion).

When you've eliminated unnecessary words and brought out the areas that lurked in vagueness in a rough draft, then read aloud what is before you. Listen for the hint of rhythm, determined not only by the beat of individual words but also by the length of your lines.

Chapter 12

The Story

The contemporary short story may not be what you think it is. Although it is the youngest of the genres, the short story has come a long way in the 150 years since it declared its independence from the novel. The short story has become shorter, for one thing, tending toward the restraint Aristotle recommended for classical drama: unity of time, place, and action. Within these narrower limits, experiments have multiplied. Writers entrust their stories to unusual narrators with distinctive voices. They work to articulate the mood of a particular situation, paying close attention to the expressiveness of style. In fact, the short story today may be more like a long poem than like the plot-centered mini-novel from which it descended.

The first step toward understanding the art of contemporary short fiction is to read its diverse practitioners. With selections culled from commercial magazines, university quarterlies, and "little" magazines, paperback anthologies of prize-winning stories are a fine place to start. You won't necessarily admire or even like everything you read, but you will begin to develop a working model to replace certain preconceived notions you may have about the genre.

Exquisite Characters

Plot is no more than footprints left in the snow after your characters have run by on their way to incredible destinations.
Ray Bradbury, "Zen in the Art of Writing: Essays on Creativity"

Short stories are not novels or full-length movies reported in brief at record-breaking pace; nor do short stories necessarily lend themselves to fictional formulae—science fiction, romance, mystery. Perhaps most important, the short story with the trick ending, perfected by O. Henry and widely anthologized in high-school textbooks, is now a formal cliché. The trick ending has been done to death in the decades since O. Henry's feckless pair of kidnappers learned *they* were going to have to pay a bratty boy's parents to take him back ("The Ransom of Red Chief") or since husband and wife discovered that she had sold her hair to buy him a watch chain while he had sold his watch to buy her a comb ("Gift of the Magi"). The surprise doesn't surprise anymore; the ingenuity has gone flat in imitation. Today, we witness the final twitchings of the O. Henry ending in such mechanical, last-minute "twists" as alarm clocks waking the narrator from a dream or revelations that the narrator is a mouse.

The point of all these negatives is this: the heart of the short story, its energy source, is not, or is no longer, the plot. As the editor of one literary quarterly expressed it for would-be contributors, what he responds to in a story above and beyond everything else is "exquisite characterization." A story is about people before it is about anything else—about human beings, richly rendered in all their quirkiness and typicality, in all their pain and pleasure, weakness and strength, despair and hope. For novice writers, then, story writing may be simpler than they thought it would be. Once they have their people, it is quite all right to make things up—astutely, of course, and honestly—as they go along. On the other hand, such open-endedness may feel scary; novice writers may prefer to devise and stick to a plot that will culminate in some definite, usually ironic ending. Where is the guarantee that traipsing through a zero-draft, following the lead of emerging characters, will get writers anywhere conclusive?

But what does "anywhere conclusive" mean? Who's to decide? There is no proper and preordained endpoint here. We must trust the characters we choose to work with and trust our ability to discover their significance. This advice may sound vague to novice writers, vague and unbelievably optimistic, as do so many attempts by seasoned writers to express the truths of their own creative experience. But again and again, these writers speak of yielding control to characters who have developed lives of their own. "I don't like the way your story ends," says reader to writer. "I wanted Maggie to quit her job and just walk away from all those people who were leaning on her." "So did I," says writer to reader, "but she just couldn't, no, wouldn't."

Once we have invented a character, we must work to give him or her autonomy and freedom. To do this, we try to feel *the character's* feelings as deeply and as accurately as we can. What this empathy often involves is rooting around in our own semiconsciousness for feelings we've suppressed, motives we don't usually acknowledge, values we certainly don't live our daily lives by. We discover the many "splits" in our sacred personality; each fragment harbors the potential life of another character. As Ray Bradbury promises, "The time will come when your characters will write your stories for you, when your emotions, free of literary cant and commercial bias, will blast the page and tell the truth."

EXERCISE: Monologue of a Past Self

Looking back on your personal development, you might define the stages you have passed through in terms of people you have been: the rebel, the do-gooder, the male chauvinist, the victim, the addict, the party animal, the loner, the born again, the kleptomaniac. Try to identify at least five different people you have been at different times in your life. Choose one, and compose a monologue, in an appropriate voice, in which you introduce and describe yourself. You may stick to actual facts, embellish them, or invent them as you wish. Don't worry about organization or repetition; just let your character ramble, including specific details as they occur—physical characteristics, likes, dislikes, habits, situations, hopes, beliefs, reminiscences. If you reach an impasse, you might try shifting to the third person and making simple statements about your character. If or when you feel like it, you can shift back to the first person.

Try reading between the lines of your monologue now. What stories might your character be trying to tell? What expectations does she or he raise? You might read this monologue aloud to your group, then sit back and listen to them speculate on possibilities for further development. What do they think your character might be about to do?

The Tension of Relationships

Ages ago in high-school English, the short story was taught by formula. All stories centered on conflict, and the challenge in reading each story was to categorize the type of conflict: did it portray Man against God, Man against Nature, Man against Society, or Man against himself? While these options may open pertinent possibilities for thematic analysis, they spell trouble for the student interested in the nuts and bolts of story making.

The "Man" part, except for its gender bias, is not so troublesome: it simply asks for a main character, something no story should be without. But what about those other big ideas—God, Nature, Society, Self—which our "Man" is supposed to struggle against? For one thing, they are too abstract. How are we supposed to translate each into a particular situation? For another, they keep pointing to a story about one beleaguered individual, maybe in the desert, maybe in the forest or a crowded mall or an empty room under a bare bulb, but always isolated, cut off from meaningful interaction with other individuals—not the best scenario for a gripping story.

One of the most frequent binds beginning writers find themselves in stems from an exclusive commitment to a single "main" character. Other characters remain flat, mere representatives, perhaps, of Society's inimicable forces or else stimuli for the main character's struggle within himself or herself. Thus whatever action the whole crew generates seems arbitrary or mechanical. There is a simple way to avoid this bind, to guarantee a story the room to expand beyond the limited consciousness of a single individual, and that is to conceive of it as the account of two characters instead of one, the account of interaction as well as action.

Students of drama recognize the importance of *two* characters in the paired terms *protagonist* and *antagonist*. However, writers don't need the mortal enmity of Antigone and Creon or Othello and Iago to make a story work. The tension that is naturally present in human relationships is quite enough: parent and child, siblings, spouses, friends, even casual acquaintances—all bonds bring potential conflicts, and the closer the relationship, often the more conflicted.

In "Last Day in the Field," by Caroline Gordon, the elderly, partly disabled narrator, Alec, ignores his better judgment: the morning after the first killing frost, he does what he has done every other year—goes bird hunting. The day brings Alec a struggle with pain and debility and, finally, a poignant acceptance of his mortality. But the story involves much more. Accompanying Alec into the field is a young man, Joe, who first spurs Alec's urges to go hunting one last time, then oversleeps. Joe doesn't do anything right. Yet Alec restrains himself from scolding or giving orders; it is more important for the older man to nurture Joe's enthusiasm and gradually channel it through expert instruction. Thus overlaid on the tension of Alec's physical ordeal in the story is a subtle interpersonal tension: between Joe, who thinks he knows everything, and Alec, the expert hunter whose time is running out, yet who manages the patience and persistence it takes to teach Joe a part of what he knows.

As you leaf through your notebook for a story idea, you might ask yourself whether the idea seems to point to a "single-character" story, and if it does, try reconceiving it to include two developed characters. For example, suppose you are considering a story based on a midwinter backpacking trip you took in the Shenandoah Mountains. Try thinking about it as an account of two friends making the trip—each with a different set of expectations. If you must go alone, imagine meeting a stranger, someone who challenges you in some way. If you can't imagine meeting a stranger, perhaps you should be thinking of the trip as a topic for a meditative poem or a personal essay.

Notice that the notion of a two-character story does not necessarily affect point of view. The impact of events may still register on only one "main" character; chances are only one "main" character will face choices and/or experience change. Yet if you are choosing first-person narration, it is all the more important to represent at least one other character besides the narrator as fully as possible—in action and dialogue—to keep the story from collapsing into tedious solipsism. Tillie Olsen's "I Stand Here Ironing" is, on the one hand, a woman's monologue about the frustration of poverty, divorce, and raising children. On the other, it's a vivid portrait of her "problem child," the daughter she mothered improperly, a dramatic analysis of failure. Similarly, the narrator of Ernest Hemingway's "In Another Country" has been deeply shaken by his experience of war, which left him physically wounded and "a little detached" from life, a little cynical. Yet the story is centered on the detached narrator's contact with an Italian major, whom circumstances have forced into even deeper cynicism.

EXERCISE: Conflicting Testimony

Choose a second character from the "outgrown selves" that you listed in the previous exercise, one that would serve as a worthy antagonist or companion to the character you developed in your monologue. Make a list of twenty "facts" about this second character, in no particular order, as they occur to you.

Next imagine a relationship between these two characters, whether well established or brand new. Let the first character give a vivid, detailed account of their first meeting, including his or her impressions of the second character and the (potential) importance of their relationship to him or her. Now let the second character present his or her version of the meeting as a rebuttal or "correction" of the first's version. Notice that the second character is in the position of having to offer proof as to why we should believe his or her account rather than the first character's.

Action

Character is Destiny.

Heraclitus

Suppose the two characters you invented in the preceding exercise got together for a day. What would they be likely to do? What sorts of things would happen to them? When you focus on such questions, you are heading into action, the other half of the story, as it were, the inevitable extension of character. Something has to occur in a story, and that something should be a little unusual, in the characters' experience if not yours. While tabloid-style death and destruction come off as cheap tricks, the everyday routines of characters (except in the hands of the most expert writers) quickly become boring.

The middle ground between holocausts or serial killings and meticulously rendered tooth-brushing or commutes to work is vast and fertile. What seeds this ground is the notion of pattern and disturbance. Often the intuition "this would make a good story" springs from a vision of disruption. If your preliminary exploration of characters lacks this spur, if you feel yourself stuck in the typical days-in-their-lives story, it is time to imagine the one day when something goes different. A Cadillac sits parked outside your mobile home when you get home from school; your new lieutenant arrives in country brimming with correctness and confidence; a smooth-talking drifter shows up at the breakfast table in your grandmother's kitchen; you receive a letter from a half-brother you didn't know you had. A story starts to grow. Notice the timing: the story *begins* with the unusual event; it doesn't save the unusual event for the finale. It's almost as if the old trick ending becomes the new point of departure. The "action" is what occurs as characters come to grips with the "trick," the tensions it causes, the choices, the change.

Characters in action are the manifestations of action in characters. What is behind this turn of phrase is *motive*. Action must appear to result from a character's plausible choices, not the author's whims. As they emerge, main characters must be allowed to develop full inner lives—they all have histories that they carry into the present, which account for their particular combination of needs, fears, hopes, actions, and reactions. The writer-creator respects and attends to these inner lives; they are crucial to the total imagined story, whether they become part of the written story or not.

Sigmund Freud, cartographer extraordinaire of the inner life, declared that where human behavior was concerned, there was no such thing as an accident. If we probed the darkest, most unconscious depths of the person(s) involved in an accidental event, we would find motives to account for it. We forget to put gas in the car the night before because we want to be late for a boring class the next day. We borrow a sweater from a sibling and then stand where a turning bus will splash us with muddy water because we want revenge. In real life, we finally squawk at such intricate explanations. Aren't there times, often important, influential, or bizarre, when we are the victims of random events? Aren't we ever capable of meaningless, indifferent activity? Probably, but such times and activities are not the stuff of stories.

Real life is much less plausible and purposeful than fiction. But then real life does not have to convince us of its "reality." (Sometimes its strangeness might disconcert us into semi-psychotic disbelief, but that's *our* problem—real life just carries on, unshaken, inescapable.) Nor does it have to please us or hold our interest. A story, on the other hand, must concentrate its resources in order to convince and engage. Thus a character's actions in a story have a logic and economy of motive that our own vague gropings and experiments never do.

EXERCISE: Motives

To get the feel for this business of motivation, look back at the "facts" you listed in the previous exercise about your second character. For each sentence of overt belief or behavior, jot down as many underlying motives as you can, as in the following two examples.

"She wears two shades of eyeshadow, black eyeliner, and thick mascara." Possible motive: she wants to hide her true self; she wants to present an artificial mask to the world, to protect her real self; she wants to annoy her father; she wants to compete with her mother; she wants to attract tough guys; she wants to be beautiful and thinks that this makeup makes her so.

"She once owned a pony that she showed with some success." Possible motive: she loves animals; she can relate to them; she *does* want responsibility, discipline, challenge; she couldn't stand the pressure from her father to win ribbons.

As you analyze your "facts," you will appreciate how complicated the issue of motivation can become. Reasons for behavior must have underlying reasons themselves; one motive gives way to a deeper one in an infinite regress. Why, for example, does this woman want to hide her true self, or annoy her father? As abstract and illusive as these explanations become, they nevertheless suggest the kind of thinking that goes on behind the scenes of a story.

Resolution

Life is a continuous series of passages, from relative innocence and ignorance to greater knowledge and experience. The short story commemorates these passages. They may be small and ordinary—a young girl realizes there are advantages to being clumsy and plain; an old gentleman recognizes that his obtuse, unpleasant neighbor is also an affectionate father. They may be bizarre and catastrophic—an intellectual is torn from his smug introversion and humiliated by a mindlessly brutal piano tuner he has allowed into his house; a woman prepares to die of a malignant brain tumor. In turn, the psychological rite of passage at the heart of all this variety gives the short story its shape.

In real life, the actions provoked by a disturbance to a pattern may go on indefinitely. In a story, on the other hand, they are focused to lead to a single crisis, a moment when one or more characters have to decide something, whether to change or not to change, whether to accept or deny. James Joyce called this moment of crisis the *epiphany*—a word rooted in the Greek verb meaning "manifest" or "show."

The stories that comprise Joyce's collection *Dubliners* suggest that epiphanies can take different forms. In one case, the end of the story offers the main character a flash of insight; his or her own true situation— the nature of his or her world and his or her place in it—manifests itself to the character. In "Araby," a boy struggles against the indifference of his family to get to a commercial bazaar, arrives just as it is closing, then realizes the vanity of his own romantic aspirations given the meanness of his environment. In the other, more frequent case, the main character is intellectually or intuitively incapable of reading manifestations, of achieving insight. Instead the final moments of the story reveal the character *to us* in all his or her limitations. Thus in "Eveline" the title character is left on a Dublin pier clinging to the departure gate, paralyzed with fear, while her would-be lover and rescuer debarks for South America.

Whether we share the main characters' final vision of themselves and their world, or we see something entirely different about them, the strong story builds toward a moment of insight that resolves, temporarily at least, the tensions created or intensified by disturbing the status quo.

The Scene

We are sealed vessels afloat upon what it is convenient to call
reality; at some moments . . . the sealing matter cracks; in
floods reality; that is a scene.

Virginia Woolf, "A Sketch of the Past"

The *scenes* of a story: these are the fiction writer's special treasure. Recall how you feel as a reader when you turn the page of a story or novel to find a dense block of print, relieved perhaps by the indentation of a paragraph or two, and you know you are in for more description or analysis or reflection. Compare that to the curiosity and heightened expectations provoked by the extra white space laced with quotation marks that announces a scene with dialogue—where you know you are going to be *shown* the created world directly instead of *told* about it.

As readers, we are most receptive to dramatic scene; yet as writers, we get caught up too often in other things, like description (of character and setting) or narration (of trivial activity). Sometimes in our enthusiasm for specific details, we forget that they are not an end in themselves, but rather the medium in which a living story can grow. And it is easier to keep on noticing and mentioning new aspects of setting, character, and activity than it is to shift into the urgencies of dialogue. For as long as we are observing the situation, amassing its external details, we are in control. If our characters are to speak, on the other hand, we must get inside them to find out what they are going to say. In other words, we must enter as participants the situation we've created as mini-gods—and anything can happen.

It is easier to remain detached from an event and offer interpretive commentaries and conclusions about it than it is to explore it from the inside, which is what we have to do if we want to portray it dramatically. Notice how the following summary avoids what might have been a challenging bit of dialogue expressing three sides of a philosophical debate:

> Charlene was beginning to fall under the spell of this strange man
> who preached brotherly love and global peace and seemed to under-
> stand Charlene's need to belong. Then Sam came back with a fistful
> of maps and dragged Charlene away.

Shying away from getting involved in a scene and acting out its parts, we sacrifice immediacy. The narrative voice drones on, interposing itself between reader and the created world of the story.

What is a scene and when should one occur? A scene is not the narration of routine activity, although a scene can occur against a backdrop of routine activity. A scene is showing instead of telling what's happening, a mini-drama with a climax, a vivid rendering of one time and one place. One brief scene might boost a paragraph of description or summary with a quick glimpse of Woolf's "reality." In Mary Hood's "Inexorable Progress," the main character's emotional deterioration seems to reverse itself after a night spent in the hospital. Yet the following summary of her recovery is subtly undercut by the too-perfect bit of dialogue with her daughter:

> Relieved, yet oddly disappointed, she went home determined to make the most of her spared life. At Sunday-night services she laid her cigarettes on the altar rail and asked for prayer to help her kick the habit. Dust gathered on the unopened conscience bottle of brandy. She built up to four miles of brisk walking every morning and was able to sleep without medication. She took up crafts, and began hooking a rug for Bonnie's room. ("Do something for yourself," Bonnie said, when her mama finished that and began a matching pillow, but Angelina said, "Doing for others, that's the reason we're here.")

At the other extreme is the scene that expands to fill the entire space of a story. For example, Hemingway's story "Hills Like White Elephants" consists of an introductory paragraph of scenic description—a rural tavern in Spain—followed by the elliptical conversation between a young man and a young woman as they wait for their train.

Dialogue

The hallmark feature of any scene, the figure in the cloth, is *dialogue*. If we look closely at the dialogue in a powerful scene, we also discern its recurring pattern, sometimes clear, sometimes camouflaged by different designs, but always there—a pattern of need. One character needs something from another character, and the second character is to some degree resistant to giving that something. At the same time, it is quite possible that the second character needs something from the first, who is similarly reluctant to yield it up. And of course the *something* is not necessarily or exclusively tangible; it may be fidelity, approval, assent, rejection, or abuse. In "Hills Like White Elephants," the pair is discussing the possibility of an abortion, though they never actually name the procedure. The young woman wants to have the baby she is carrying and marry the man; she wants to believe this option could produce a "happy ending." The young man wants her to go through with the abortion; he wants to believe that they can return to the innocent freedom he thought they enjoyed before the pregnancy. Their talk goes around and around. If you imagined a dialogue as a product of the second exercise in this chapter, you might see a similar pattern of conflicting intangible needs emerge in the desire of both characters to be right, to provide the definitive version of an event. When a scene portrays more than two characters in conversation, the need vectors begin to define even more complicated and subtle patterns of tension.

The cause of a scene, then, is also its purpose. Scenes exist in order to present (and discover) conflicting needs. "Follow intensity," Carol Bly advises would-be writers in a book with a wonderfully intense title: *The Passionate, Accurate Story.* In other words, seek out the moments of tension and then render them in the most tension-enhancing form: the scene. Created characters themselves will often initiate scenes if given a little freedom; the seasoned writer can almost feel them pressing for the opportunity to act out some judgment or event mentioned by the narrative voice. The beginning writer may need to approach the question of scene more analytically, studying paragraphs of narration for statements that could produce the reaction "*Wait* a minute! It couldn't have been *that* easy." The near-spellbound Charlene must have put up a little resistance when Sam tried to drag her away from the charismatic stranger.

How about the sentence "Before Charlene left for the mall to meet her friends, she got her allowance from her father"? If obtaining her allowance every week is effortless for Charlene, that fact may not be worth mentioning; if, on the other hand, it often provokes a confrontation about what she is or isn't doing to help around the house, that confrontation cries out to be rendered in more detail, maybe not a full-blown scene but a brief dip into the "reality" of *he said*'s and *she said*'s in order to convey the quality of Charlene's life. The story writer's rule of thumb about conflict and tension is this: if you're just going to gloss over it, forget it—leave it out. If you feel you can't leave it out, it's time to downshift from telling gear into showing gear and create a scene. Notice in the following example that this shift in mode from summary to scene would mean some expansion, but not necessarily pages and pages.

> Before she put on her makeup and moussed her hair, Charlene slouched down to the basement room where her father was laboring over another of his ship models. Trying not to breathe the thick smoke too deeply, she asked, "Do you suppose I could have part of my allowance?"
>
> Her father puffed on the cigarette hanging from the corner of his mouth and fiddled with the delicate rigging. "What do you think?" he answered, never lifting his eyes from the ship.
>
> There was silence.
>
> "It's pretty," Charlene said finally.

Her father straightened up, looked her over. "Pretty?" he said. Charlene hunched her shoulders up to her ears. Her father blew a long blast of smoke. "My wallet's up on my dresser."

Dialogue is what gives scenes their life, and dialogue requires tension. If the tension relaxes, the scene goes limp and dies. In this respect, good dialogue is not necessarily "realistic." While it may be true that in real life we speak out of need, it is also true that our needs are not always urgent or specific; nor do they always meet with resistance. In real life, the question "Could we meet on Saturday instead of Sunday?" may ask nothing more than that. In that case, however, it doesn't belong in written dialogue.

Real people, by and large, don't have the naïveté or the courage to say aloud those things that have to be said to keep a story moving. Real people learn conventions of polite behavior; they often talk only out of the need to fill up silence or make conversation, while their more problematic needs remain undifferentiated and deeply buried. One thing distinguishes created characters from real people: their buried selves gradually come unburied; subtext becomes text. That's what stories are about.

Your invented characters, in other words, begin to cut through rote convention; that is part of earning their leading roles. They must be worthy of being written about. When they are summoned center stage to engage each other in dialogue, the urgencies of subtext energize their performance. In the story "Fenstad's Mother," by Charles Baxter, the first words we hear mother say to son are "How's your soul?" In the story "The Island," by Alistair Macleod, a woman meets a strange man whose fourth, and unprompted, statement to her is "Some people are lonely no matter where they are."

EXERCISE: Dialogue

Imagine yourself in an encounter with someone important to you yet whom you do not fully trust, someone with whom you are aware of "playing a role." Teachers and students, parents and children, friends and would-be lovers, bosses and employees: there are few relationships in which we do not hide some part of ourselves for purposes of safety, efficiency, or simply convenience. Let the initial subject of conversation between you and this other person be neutral: an assignment, future plans, a past anecdote, even the time or the weather. Notice that once in motion, the conversation will drift away from this subject as each speaker responds to the response of the other.

Divide your page in half vertically. On the left side, record the dialogue, alternating speakers. On the right side, jot down what you imagine each of you is actually thinking as you contribute to the flow of conversation. How might the buried material on the right begin gradually to shape the spoken material on the left? What would happen if one of you all at once articulated this subtext? You might prefer to try this exercise with the two characters you created earlier in this chapter.

●   ●   ●

Characters don't temporize the way real people do: greeting each other, standing around inquiring after each other's health, making dental appointments, or asking what's for dinner. Nor do they take up precious time and attention telling each other things they both already know or asking each other rhetorical questions simply in order to get the information to the reader, as do the characters below:

> "I can't believe it's been six months since you dropped by my house-warming," she said. "You know, I'm still enjoying that gloxinia you brought."

> "You know you get so nervous you can't even think straight when you wait till the last minute to study chemistry," I told him, "and this is your last chance to pull a passing grade in the course."

> "How does it feel to move to our small midwestern town after living in Paris for all those years?" she asked.

While there is certainly tension implicit in these remarks, it gets diffused by the factual exposition. Better to handle this exposition through summary or implication and allow the characters to ask more naturally, "How long has it been?"; "When are you going to hit the books?"; "Do you like it here?"

Dialogue, then, furnishes the means by which characters face their differences, their issues, their conflicting needs. This is not to say that they may not talk about dentists and dinner; but those subjects will become the terms for a subtle pushing and pulling. Nor is this to say that your characters must never experience a conflict-free moment; it just isn't a good idea to waste dialogue on it unless, of course, it is the hard-won relaxing of tension that precedes the silence of the end.

Time Management

The world the story writer creates is by definition a world of *time,* a world of events organized by chronology, of characters with histories, of effects preceded by causes, of long, slow curves before the fast breaks. The lyric poem, by contrast, celebrates the timeless. "The sonnet," proclaimed the nineteenth-century poet Dante Gabriel Rossetti, "is a moment's monument." But for the story writer, time is inescapable, stubborn, ever threatening to bog him or her down.

Suppose, for example, that you have begun to draft the story that emerged at the start of this chapter about the backpacking trip in the Shenandoah Mountains. Vaguely, but with some excitement, you can foresee the stranger who will cross the path of an innocent suburbanite in the wilderness, but before you can begin to develop the details of this unknown character and learn exactly what will happen when the two people meet, you may feel that you should introduce the young protagonist and somehow convey something of the twenty years that have shaped him or her. That accomplished, you must still get the person up and out of the house, with equipment packed, and across the necessary miles, by car and foot, to the point of the meeting. All that takes creative energy—so much that when the two people are finally eye to eye, you may be so tired of slogging through time that you are ready to quit.

It often takes the experience of one or two false starts to decide to *begin* the story with the meeting, but that is one way to keep time from getting the upper hand. As one student aptly advised another, "Begin with a good part and stick with the good parts." In other words, the sooner the significant disturbance occurs, the better. In the case of the backpacker, this means identifying the main action—a scene or series of scenes that vaguely excite you, even though you don't necessarily know the story's form or outcome. Then through significant detail, gesture, and passing remark, you can weave into the story any important information that was loaded into the discarded prologue of preparations. What the protagonist is wearing, what he or she is in the process of doing when he or she meets up with the stranger, who speaks first, how he or she introduced himself or herself—all can be made to carry implications.

In general, the good parts are the scenes, wired with tension, and sticking with scenes means keeping time on our side. In a scene, imagined time, or the time it ostensibly takes for the dialogue and action to take place, comes closest to "real" time, or the time it actually takes to read through a scene. John Updike's frequently anthologized story "A & P," for instance, begins with the moment the adolescent Sammy, a supermarket checker at a beach resort, first catches sight of three girls in bathing suits in his store. As he performs his duties at his cash register, he watches their progress up and down the aisles. The story ends when his manager asks the girls to leave because they are not adequately dressed, and Sammy, in a gesture of futile chivalry, takes off his apron and quits. The story consists of one sustained vivid scene in the present. It took perhaps twenty imaginary minutes to happen; it takes twenty real minutes to read. For the beginning writer, there are advantages of clarity and momentum in this simple management of time.

Suppose your story must take place over a longer stretch of time in order to portray more gradual change. Still, you'd best conceive of it as a series of scenes, episodes of action and interaction that side by side will show growth or deterioration. How to dispose of the time between scenes? White space. The skipping of a few lines to show some passage of time— called a *narrative break*—is an indispensable device for the contemporary story writer. It works as a bridge over the mire of irrelevant details, leading us from one intense spot to another. One word of caution, though, because the narrative break can be misused: you may catch yourself skipping over an emotionally or technically difficult scene to a later, more manageable moment, sometimes referring to the phantom scene of crisis by means of a bloodless *flashback*. In general, unless you are making a deliberate technical decision to downplay it, a crisis needs to occur onstage, not during an intermission.

Flashbacks are a temptation to avoid. You may have generated much of the material in a zero-draft by a sort of flashing back—allowing your imagination to loop into the past in order to gather key details, incidents, and missing clues to the puzzle you are piecing together in the story's present. Once you have filled in all the gaps, invented or recalled all the pertinent facts and events, weigh carefully the disadvantages of actual flashbacks before consciously choosing to use them in a finished work.

Readers commit themselves emotionally to the main time frame a narrative establishes. Flashbacks to earlier time frames break the momentum of the story because they ask readers to be patient while you suspend the action in order to fill in background. Sometimes a brief dip into the past can give a moment in the main time frame richness and depth. In those instances, it is important to signal the shift to an earlier time ("Years ago, when his mother was still alive . . ."), as well as the return to the main one ("Now, as he wonders whether to stay or go . . ."). And all the while, remember that readers are waiting.

Notice that flashbacks reverse the compression of time in fiction that the convention of the narrative break makes possible: prolonged flashbacks expand an imagined time of minutes into actual reading time of perhaps hours, like the proverbial drowning man whose whole lifetime flashes instantly through his mind. This warping may be an effect we are looking for in our narrative; so might be a certain fragmentation of chronology. A particular narrator might be plagued by flashbacks. But more often than flashbacks solve narrative problems, they get out of hand. Before we know it, we've got flashbacks within flashbacks, a confusing narrative, and frustrated readers. The most effective narrative strategy strikes a balance between the need to begin with intensity (the disturbance) and the need to begin at the chronological beginning. Then with astutely rationed references to past times, it moves steadily forward.

Chapter 13

The Essay

The essay is a pair of baggy pants into which nearly anyone and anything can fit.

Joseph Epstein, "Writing Essays"

Imagination is not the special gift of novelists, poets, sculptors, and painters but resides in all of us and defines us as human. So declares the biologist and philosopher Jacob Bronowski, who identifies the ability "to make images and to move them about inside one's head in new arrangements" as "the common root from which science and literature both spring and grow and flourish together."

If the spinning of images exists at the heart of all creative thinking, both artistic and scientific, why is it so often discouraged in professional nonfiction writing? Physicists and mathematicians, those lovers of the abstract and the analytical, resort to image and anecdote to represent a reality that would be otherwise inarticulable or indeterminate. Historians, social scientists, and literary scholars perpetually weave disjointed information into coherent stories. Yet the college curriculum isolates "creative" writing from all other forms of academic writing, implying that its imaginative activities should occur only in specialized courses, and that nowhere else do we ever tell stories, paint pictures, invent metaphors, or manipulate perspectives. While the technical essays that fill professional journals may achieve an efficient shorthand to report methodology and data, their attempts at depersonalizing content and eliminating ambiguity at all costs suit only the narrowest of purposes, the most limited of audiences, and the most specialized of "truths."

In the last twenty years, nonfiction writers have staked out an infinitely wider and more fertile territory. Journalists, travel writers, scientists and social scientists, physicians, biographers and autobiographers,

160

historians, satirists—all have laid claim in their essays to creative writing. They revitalize language with fresh metaphors, paint vivid images, and often surprise readers with their startling juxtapositions. They tell stories, create scenes, and interpolate dialogue. They attend to matters of shape, striving for energetic beginnings, rich, coherent middles, and well-earned ends. In other words, they continually tap the resources of the imagination to discover and express what they know.

If all these resemblances establish the contemporary essay as legitimate sibling to the poem and story, then how is it different? Poems play with the poetic line; stories create narrators and entire micro-worlds. What gives the essay its distinctive individuality? The answer to this question begins with the author—the observing, remembering, analyzing, commenting, and persuading "I" at the essay's source.

Authority

Essays . . . hang somewhere on a line between two sturdy poles: this is what I think, and this is what I am.
    Edward Hoagland, "What I Think, What I Am"

Each poem creates its special persona, or speaker; in a story, the narrative voice is an extension of the invented world. In the personal essay, on the other hand, we assume that the author is speaking to us directly about thoughts and events. While poets and fiction writers experiment with diverse personae and narrative strategies, a collection of essays by the same author more often strikes us by its consistency of style and voice, evidence of the single sensibility at its source.

Despite its periodic dalliances with objectivity, logic, and "pure reason" that began in the eighteenth century, the essay has remained faithful to the personal—open-ended and speculative. The word *essay* itself derives from the French verb meaning "try" and emphasizes the peculiarly provisional quality of its contents. A glance at some classic titles suggests the same quality: from Montaigne's "Of Cannibals," through Charles Lamb's "A Chapter on Ears," to George Orwell's "Reflections on Gandhi" and James Baldwin's "Notes of a Native Son." The tentativeness of these titles should not mislead us into expecting haphazard structure or inconclusive observations. Each writer has a point to make, but, as a title may willingly admit, it is one writer's point based on one writer's thoughts and experiences—not the final, all-encompassing word.

As essayists, then, we write as ourselves about our experience of the real world and what it has caused us to feel and think. But because our material is the communal reality to which everyone lays claim, our basic concern is a unique one. As poets and fiction writers, we try to seduce our readers into believing in our created worlds; as essayists, we must convince readers to believe in *us*. We must establish our authority to speak about the real world even though we may know only our one small part. As Henry David Thoreau suggests in his opening chapter to *Walden*, the essay's authority is grounded in the "personal":

> We commonly do not remember that it is, after all, always the first person that is speaking. I should not talk so much about myself if there were any body else whom I knew as well.

Thoreau goes on to encourage his readers to "accept such portions as apply to them," trusting that "none will stretch the seams in putting on the coat, for it may do good service to him whom it fits."

Authority can be embellished by flashy means, such as dazzling style or wacky humor. But in the end, it depends on two things: originality of viewpoint and potency of evidence. The intense subjectivity and the richness of sensory detail so crucial to all powerful writing serve a special purpose in the essay, where the reader already assumes the reality of the world we are writing about but may question the legitimacy and value of our comments about it. If we rely on vague generalizations about a topic like patriotism or racism, our readers will wind up doubting not the existence of these issues but rather our right and ability to say anything meaningful about them. We won't appear to know any more than our readers already know—public platitudes, typical attitudes. Who will care?

If, on the other hand, we begin to recreate the neighborhood chauvinism of our school days, our readers pay attention. Details (sensory images, facts, anecdotes, quotations) convince readers that we have something new and interesting to say.

In his essay "What Is Patriotism?" the economist Stanley Sheinbaum approaches this big buzzword through a telling personal recollection:

> I was but a lad when the kids on the next block, 124th Street, and those on 123rd, mine, waged war with each other, complete with hostile invasions and even injuries. "Us kids" on 123rd Street were always the good ones, of course, always described to our mamas and papas as the defenders, never the aggressors like "them." I remember asking myself, What the hell is all this about? What's better about 123rd Street? While I knew a little about architecture at the time, I was never impressed that the buildings on either block outdid those on the other. Nor did I know much more about girls at the time, but even my untutored eye could not discern any difference between the

good looks on my block and theirs. So what was I expected to be loyal to on 123rd Street?

With the homely specifics of this anecdote, Sheinbaum brings a powerful abstraction down to earth and insinuates the controversial point he will make explicit later on: patriotism is a flame fanned by national leaders in order to manipulate their childlike followers.

In the essay "Night Walker," Brent Staples presents an unexpected perspective on racism, beginning with an almost palpably concrete scene:

> My first victim was a woman—white, well dressed, probably in her early 20s. I came upon her late one evening on a deserted street in Hyde Park, a relatively affluent neighborhood in an otherwise mean, impoverished section of Chicago. As I swung onto the avenue behind her, there seemed to be a discreet, uninflammatory distance between us. Not so. She cast back a worried glance. To her, the youngish black man—a broad six feet two inches with a beard and billowing hair, both hands shoved in the pockets of a bulky military jacket—seemed menacingly close. She picked up her pace and was soon running in earnest. Within seconds she disappeared into a cross street.

Staples's details—his "victim," the setting, and interestingly, a vivid shot of the author himself—establish his unusual, but inarguable perspective: he has earned authority.

EXERCISE: Playing the Expert

We are all authorities on our life histories—hence the essay's slant toward autobiography, the journal entry, the letter, the memoir. When not relying on personal narrative for authority, the essayist often draws on expertise, a body of knowledge or experience that will both distinguish and validate a chosen perspective.

Make a list of at least ten areas in which you might like to claim expertise. Remember the trivial, perhaps ridiculous possibilities (playing computer games, cutting weight before a wrestling match) as well as the more serious (a profession or hobby, a disability). Remember too that you can be an expert on a certain kind of failure (an inability to speak in large groups, difficulty in understanding men, women, children, doctors, lawyers, professors, athletes, and so on).

Don't worry about the objective validity of your claim, but choose one of these areas that seems most interesting to you and make a second list of at least ten facts or experiences that might establish your authority to speak about it. Notice that simply citing titles or prizes will not do the trick. You may be the captain of the gymnastics team or a master gardener, but your reader won't believe either one unless you recreate through sensory detail the concrete experiences to prove it—the feel of the balance beam under your bare feet, the texture of compost. Notice too that you can check back through your notebook for items that suit either list.

Finally, jot down one conclusion to which your "expertise" has led you, preferably one that goes against the grain of prevailing wisdom on your subject or gives a twist to common knowledge. Explain your viewpoint in a paragraph or two, introducing appropriate details from your second list. When you read these brief writings aloud to your group, ask their impression of your authority. Do they think you come across as someone credible with something special to say? You may wish to develop your subject at more length—in other words, write an essay.

Audience

To emphasize the issue of authority in the essay is to acknowledge the power of the *audience* that grants it. Sometimes the essayist plays protagonist to an antagonistic audience, or vice versa. At other times, a sense of audience hovers in the back of the essayist's mind as he or she writes, like the Hindu god whose unnamed absence implies general presence. But always audience exerts its influence as something the essay must not only identify but also shape and change.

A fiction writer might sketch a homeless woman on a park bench because setting, characters, and events demand her presence; she adds a vivid thread to the story's texture. A poet might describe the same woman in order to explore a complex response to her plight. While the essayist also strives for vividness in images and authenticity in response, his or her further concern is with the persuasive impact of the presentation on an audience. The essayist is conscious that he or she, the audience, and the subject—the homeless woman—all inhabit the same public world. What writer thinks and feels, reader might also be led to think and feel.

Thus, if often subtly, the essayist presses the audience to do more than simply take in a subject. The same details that validate authority are selected to provoke a judgment, one that agrees with the writer's. Himself the writer of many essays, Edward Hoagland admits "the essayist, however cleverly he camouflages his intentions, is a bit of a teacher or reformer." To perform these roles successfully, the essayist must postulate an audience: minds to change and reform.

Both Norman Mailer and Norman Cousins composed essays in response to the death of the boxer Benny Paret at the gloves of his opponent in the ring, Emile Griffith. The former writer was moved to tribute by the event; the latter, to outrage. Both marshal a selection of details in order to validate themselves and their responses. Both assume a particular audience, but very different ones. Interestingly, these different audiences are just as influential as the authors' opposing viewpoints in determining each essay's strategy and shape.

In "The Death of Benny Paret," Mailer writes for the boxing fan, someone who understands that taking "three punches to the head in order to give back two" is an admirable and cunning strategy. He assumes an audience who believes that an insult to one's masculinity may not excuse punching the insulter to death, but at least it explains such an act. Mailer focuses on the individual athletes, their talents as boxers, and their motivations. In the end, his diction and imagery press his audience to regard Paret as he does, as a sort of hero, memorable, a little larger than life.

> Paret died on his feet. As he took those eighteen punches, something happened to everyone who was in psychic range of the event. Some part of his death reached out to us. One felt it hover in the air. He was still standing in the ropes, trapped as he had been before, he gave some little half-smile of regret, as if he were saying, "I didn't know I was going to die just yet," and then, his head leaning back but still erect, his death came to breathe about him. He began to pass away. As he passed, so his limbs descended beneath him, and he sank slowly to the floor. He went down more slowly than any fighter had ever gone down, he went down like a large ship which turns on end and slides second by second into its grave.

The reader beyond "psychic range of the event" will probably remain there, skeptical of the heroic scale of this description and profoundly disturbed by the sound of Griffith's punches "like a heavy ax in the distance chopping into a wet log."

Norman Cousins's title, "Who Killed Benny Paret?" establishes a more confrontational relationship with his audience. At the same time, he assumes a more general audience—readers who are not captivated by boxing and may thus be receptive to his more universal, humanistic appeal. Cousins's focus is the politics of boxing, a chain of profit and influence in which the boxers are faceless and powerless pawns. His appeal is to facts rather than "personal interest." The entire Mailer essay becomes one paragraph in Cousins's:

> Recently a young man by the name of Benny Paret was killed in the ring. The killing was seen by millions; it was on television. In the

twelfth round he was hit hard in the head several times, went down, was counted out, and never came out of the coma.

Interestingly, his most lyrical writing is lavished not on the dying boxer, but on the human brain,

> the most delicate and complex mechanism in all creation. It has a lacework of millions of highly fragile nerve connections. Nature attempts to protect this exquisitely intricate machinery by encasing it in a hard shell. Fortunately, the shell is thick enough to withstand a great deal of pounding. Nature, however, can protect man against everything except man himself.

In this passage, Cousins assumes, or hopes for, an audience capable of becoming tender and emotional—of acknowledging not the grandness of a fighter going down forever but the fragile treasure in our almost-as-fragile skulls that sustains our lives. He is aiming at the reader who doesn't support boxing but doesn't have anything against it either. In the following passage, he wants to give that reader something against it.

> It is nonsense to talk about prize fighting as a test of boxing skills. No crowd was ever brought to its feet screaming and cheering at the sight of two men beautifully dodging and weaving out of each other's jabs. The time the crowd comes alive is when a man is hit hard over the heart or the head, when his mouthpiece flies out, when blood squirts out of his nose or eyes, when he wobbles under the attack and his pursuer continues to smash at him with poleax impact.

EXERCISE: Playing to the House

As an essayist, the audience you assume influences many of your technical choices: style, tone, and selection and deployment of detail. Consider the opinion you expressed in the previous exercise and the details you relied on to earn your authority. Does that piece of writing imply an audience? To whom does it appeal, a reader who is just like you but lacks knowledge of the one topic you are addressing? Too often, beginning essayists unconsciously write for themselves, and because they already know their subjects and agree with their own ideas, they might have trouble imagining what is intriguing, difficult, or controversial about their topics.

The tension generated by an adversarial audience can give an essay a positive "edge." Imagine revising your paragraph(s) for a reader who thinks he or she is also a sort of expert on your subject or at your activity and is ready to disagree with your presentation of it. Jot down some things you would do differently. Now imagine a reader who believes your subject or activity is an utterly worthless pursuit. Jot down details or strategies you might turn to in order to reach that audience.

How might you alter your paragraph(s) in order to appeal to a young child? a reader who is terminally ill? a reader who is serving a ten-year term in prison? Would you compose it differently for an all-male or an all-female audience? Choose from among these possible audiences (or other unusual readers that you invent) the one that requires the most reshuffling of your original strategy. Then try rewriting your paragraph(s) appropriately.

Transitions

A number of essay conventions have evolved from the close relationship between author and audience: verbal ways for the essayist to look back over a shoulder and ask of readers, "Are you following me?" The most pervasive of these is the habit of telling as well as showing, offering commentary on the evidence along with (and often before) the evidence. This technique, which can tear the sensuous fabric of a poem and destroy illusion in a story, is, according to Edward Hoagland, welcome in the essay, where mind speaks to mind.

The skilled essayist senses when readers need the sensory grounding of an example and when they are ready for interpretive summary; when they need the emotional appeal of narrative to deepen their understanding and when they need the intellectual focus of an abstract idea. Thus, in developing his viewpoint on patriotism, Sheinbaum expands his scope from a reminiscence about childhood to a rather global generalization: "We have known for centuries that propagandistic rhetoric and the waving of the flag alongside militaristic adventurism evoke 'proud' emotional stirrings, and we convince ourselves that we are functioning on some higher plane."

With similar shifts, Staples develops his essay about "night walking," allowing his own frustrating, frightening experiences to speak eloquently for themselves, then stepping away from them to offer flashes of poignant analysis concerning "the unwieldy inheritance" he'd come into—"the ability to alter public space in ugly ways."

> Women are particularly vulnerable to street violence, and young black males are drastically overrepresented among the perpetrators of that violence. Yet these truths are no solace against the alienation that comes of being ever the suspect, an entity with whom pedestrians avoid making eye contact.

The continuous movement back and forth from specific instance to general significance, from fact to meaning, from the sensory and emotional to the intellectual—such is the art of the essay. This movement can also lead to problems in this audience-friendly genre, however. Without the rhythm of the poetic line, and often without the chronology that structures the story, the essay can become disjointed and difficult for readers to follow. White space and breaks in the poem and story generate tension and maintain intensity. In the essay, these blanks can produce confusion and unwanted ambiguity, and so the essayist is careful to fill them in by providing *transitions*.

A basic way to ease transition is to incorporate into the lead sentence of one paragraph an important word from the final sentence of the previous paragraph. After commenting on his first experience as an inadvertently menacing "night walker," Staples consolidates his ideas and ups the ante for the paragraphs to follow: "I soon gathered that being perceived as dangerous is a hazard in itself: Where fear and weapons meet—and they often do in urban America—there is always the possibility of death."

The next paragraph picks up the focus on fear before it moves into a fresh burst of examples: "In that first year, my first away from my hometown, I was to become thoroughly familiar with the language of fear."

Succeeding paragraphs set the seamless background for further concrete experiences:

> I moved to New York nearly two years ago and I have remained an avid night walker. In central Manhattan, the near-constant crowd covers the tense one-on-one street encounters. Elsewhere, things can get very taut indeed.
> After dark, on the warrenlike streets of Brooklyn where I live, I often see women who fear the worst from me.

The repeated idea of fear-intensity-tautness threads these sentences into a tight sequence that is reinforced by careful designations of time and place: *soon, that first year, two years ago, after dark, New York, Manhattan, elsewhere, Brooklyn.*

EXERCISE: Smoothing Transitions

Many personal essays record variations on a theme. The theme may be a person, a place, an object, or an idea; it may be a particular event or chain of events. The essayist places it in different contexts, contemplates it from different distances, turns it inside out and upside down.

The strongest essays enlist a wealth of transitional words and phrases to clarify the nature and purpose of each variation. Sparing the multi-syllabic transitions of formal prose (*therefore, moreover, furthermore, however*), try adding to the following friendly list of ways to alert readers to shifts in direction, distance, and scope: *by the way, on the one hand . . . on the other hand, similarly, in other words, for example, for instance, in general, actually, meanwhile.*

Go back to the areas of expertise you listed in the first exercise in this chapter, choose another study or activity from the list, and compose a concrete sentence or two about the last time you engaged in it. For example: "The peas I planted last week have not yet appeared and may have been washed away by the rain." Compose a sequence of nine or ten sentences to follow this lead, beginning each with a transitional phrase from your list and allowing the meaning of the sentence to be shaped accordingly. Introduce your first three additions with these three signals, in this order:

In general
For example (or for instance)
But

Don't worry about the relevance of what you produce; enjoy following your own somewhat arbitrary directions. Just as a poet may let the sounds of words dictate which are chosen, the essayist can wander among ideas, allowing transitions to lead the way. Play a variation on the proverbial pilot who doesn't have any idea where he's going but is at least making good time. You may not know your destination, but equipped with your favorite transitions your course will be smooth and the visibility clear.

Thesis

Knowledge is not made out of knowledge. Knowledge swims up from invention and imagination—from ardor—and sometimes even an essay can invent, burn, guess, try out, dig up, hurtle forward, succumb to that flood of sign and nuance that adds up to intuition, disclosure, discovery. The only nonfiction worth writing—at least for me—lacks the summarizing gift, is heir to nothing, and sets out with empty pockets from scratch.

Cynthia Ozick, "Art and Ardor"

From high school on, many student writers have been taught to compose essays according to a closed model, one that would probably suffocate any creative thinker who writes as Joan Didion does: "to find out what I'm thinking, what I'm looking at, what I see and what it means." The ideal essay according to this model takes a position (its *thesis*) and argues it with logic and economy; sensory detail serves as evidence to prove the case irrefutably.

While students are still struggling with outlines and thesis statements and airtight conclusions, contemporary essayists have broken the spell of objective truth and left behind the imaginary courtroom with its verdicts of true and false, right and wrong, win and lose. They hold up to our eyes and minds not an absolute, unassailable principle, but rather a portion of life, richly and creatively rendered, and their own provisional commentary.

With the flowering in the 1960s of "new journalism," for example, came the realization that every reporter and every publication finally reconstructs only a partial view of events. Instead of one news story that reports the *truth,* there are as many true stories of an event as there are individuals touched by it.

If it were your task to write about the life of American POW's in World War II, would you summarize official government records? interview survivors of Nazi camps in Germany? summarize the writings of those who suffered the long and deadly march in the Philippines under Japanese captors? Would you tell the story, instead, of loyal, hard-working Japanese-Americans interned by a racist nation in the throes of a frightening war? Each of these possibilities would lead to different conclusions and different, possibly contradictory, visions of truth. One's account of tyranny is another's account of necessary discipline. One's record of a humiliating childhood experience is another's youthful prank. Although claims of truth traditionally cling to nonfiction, the essayist strives for the truth of individual testimony rather than some abstract, omniscient conclusion.

All this is to downplay the importance of the thesis in the creative essay. How many times in an essay by Russell Baker or Annie Dillard or Lewis Thomas do we search in vain for a thesis in the place where we were taught it should be, at the end of the first paragraph? How many times do we fail to find an explicit thesis statement at all? How many times has a wonderful essay opened up many more issues than its apparent thesis has addressed and closed? The life of the essay can often exemplify a truth of which a thesis statement is only a crude approximation.

To dismiss the traditional thesis is not to recommend "pointlessness" or a lack of unity in the essay. But as with the theme of a poem or a story, the real point or unifying idea of a creative essay is discovered in the process of drafting it. It may emerge from the scraps of notes and first-draft freewriting as a question, a telling image, or a clear insight or feeling. A unifying idea offers something to hold on to through the phases of revision; a criterion that determines what gets cut, altered, or expanded. But it may never be reducible, even by the author, to a simple proposition. Edward Hoagland claims for the personal essay the same integrity we attribute to poems and stories. It won't "boil down to a summary." And though "it contains a point which is its real center," that point "couldn't be uttered in fewer words than the essayist has used."

In her essay from *The Moon by Whale Light*, Diane Ackerman describes in lush imagery the icebergs she and the crew of her *Zodiac* pass as they travel from ship to shore:

> Icebergs are not always smooth. Many have textures—waffle patterns, pockmarks—and some look pounded by Near Eastern metalsmiths. One newly calved iceberg lies like a chunk of glass honeycomb, spongy from being underwater. (At some point, it was other side up.) Another has beautiful blue ridges like muscles running along one flank. So many icelets thicken the water, each one quivering with sparkle, that the sea looks like aluminum foil being shaken in the sun. There are baths of ice with blue lotion, ice grottoes, ice curled round like the fleecy pelt of a lamb, razor-backed ice, sixteen swans on an ice merry-go-round, ice pedestals, ice combs, ice dragons with ice wings spread, an ice garden where icebergs grow and die, ice tongs with blue ice between their claws, an ice egret stretching ice wings and a long, rippling ice neck out of the water. Apricot light spills over distant snowcapped mountains. Wedges of peppermint blue ice drift past. Behind us the *Zodiac* leaves a froth like white petticoats. And farther behind, dark shapes arch out of the water—penguins feeding, oblivious of what we call beauty.

In her obsessive fidelity to her subject, Ackerman wrests the truth of this experience, a truth that involves the wonder of human beings confronting an awesome, alien environment. The point of Ackerman's paragraph is implied in every element of its extravagant texture. The rich excess of imagery suggests that it is the writer, determined to convey the quality of her experience, who actually creates the experience. Her language transforms a distant, strange, monochromatic world into a place of more familiar beauty, movement, color. As William Blake observed, "Where Man is not Nature is barren." Meanwhile, the oblivious penguins feed.

Essay As Journey/Journey As Essay

Essays are journeys. When you write an essay, you are a traveler. You might try a scenic route through a familiar subject or pick your tentative way through a less familiar one and then invite the reader along with your writing as a guide. Just as the chronology of narrative lends its order to the essay, so too does the spatial metaphor of a mental journey.

Journeys are essays, attempts at something new. They may be explorations, adventures, recreations, pilgrimages, or escapes, but they all involve leaving home. The traveler may depart nervous and naïve but return an authority, fortified with original anecdotes about confronting the unexpected and unknown, as well as with plenty of snapshots, or perhaps a video, capturing the concrete details of the trip.

As this metaphor suggests, there is a natural relationship between a physical "essay" (like a journey) and the verbal essay—a relationship that gives birth to the popular travel essay. The subject of travel is perfectly suited to the technique of the essay. It pits the author's sensibility against foreign forces that will challenge it in new and unexpected ways. Thus tension is inevitable, as well as the emergence of interesting "points." In addition, the travel essay assumes an audience unfamiliar with its locale(s), with no "share" in its reality, and thus more willing to grant its author authority based simply on abundant and exotic detail.

The passage by Ackerman illustrates the importance of sensory detail to travel writing, in which the author must act as intermediary between alien setting and audience, pushing his or her imaginative resources to the limit to capture the setting's full truth. In the following introduction to his essay "El Dorado," Evan Connel lavishes a similar passion on concrete description, straining words and syntax to convey the mind-boggling spectacle of Musica gold. Notice, by the way, the contrast between the opening clause, a pale summary of his topic, and the specific details that erupt after it.

> If you go to Bogotá and visit the Banco de la República you will see, in the bank's Museo del Oro, nearly 10,000 pre-Columbian gold artifacts: labrets, nose rings, brooches, masks, spoons, pincers, receptacles, representations of birds, snakes, crocodiles, people, animals. You walk down a corridor lined on both sides with display cases, each case packed with these opulent creations. You turn right, walk down another corridor past more of the same. Then more. And more. Finally, instead of going out, you are led into a dark room. After you have been there awhile the lights begin rising so gradually that you expect to hear violins, and you find yourself absolutely surrounded by gold. If all of Tut's gold were added to this accumulation, together with everything Schliemann plucked from Mycenae and Hissarlik, you could scarcely tell the difference.

EXERCISE: Travelogue

Keeping in mind the passages by Ackerman and Connel as models, take your notebook with you on a trip to a place that you have never been before. The journey can be distant and long, across borders or seas, if you are fortunate enough to be planning one. More likely you will have to settle for a nearby city, mountain, or beach; a part of town; a building on campus; a park or museum; or even a mall that you have never visited. The important thing is to frame your expedition as a journey into the unknown, and your writing as an attempt to convey a sense of place to an untraveled audience, primarily by means of vivid and captivating detail.

Once you have gathered an abundance of observations and impressions, try drafting this material into a short essay, adapting some of the tricks of organization Ackerman and Connel use. Both writers, for example, slip into lists in order to pack a rich diversity of data into a few sentences. Notice how both writers translate a spatial experience into a written coherence: Ackerman's images and transitional words seem to follow the sweep of her eyes; Connel's walk us through a museum tour. Notice how repetition unifies the iceberg passage, and how both writers vary their sentence patterns for emphasis.

The Manifesto

The essay's many-rooted equation always links two central but volatile variables: an author who is onto something new and an audience willing to be interested. Besides the travel essay, another of the essay's natural evolutions is the *manifesto*—a public declaration of intentions and principles by a self-appointed authority.

The history of literature has always included a tradition of specialized manifestos: attempts to define the nature of true literary art, under what circumstances it is produced, by whom, and/or to what purpose. Aristotle in his *Poetics* derived general rules for the drama from the specific works of ancient Greek playwrights; his principle of unity of time, place, and action is still relevant to the issue of aesthetic form. In the eighteenth century, Alexander Pope's *Essay on Criticism* offered this neat encouragement to the writer uncertain of his or her special gifts:

> True wit is Nature to advantage dress'd,
> What oft was thought, but ne'er so well expressed. . . .
> True ease in writing comes from art, not chance,
> As those move easiest who have learn'd to dance.

In the Preface to his *Lyrical Ballads,* William Wordsworth sheds light on the interplay of inspiration and deliberation that defines the creative process: "Poetry is the spontaneous overflow of powerful feelings: it takes its origin from emotion recollected in tranquillity." Echoed by other poets of the Romantic period, Samuel Taylor Coleridge, Percy Bysshe Shelley, and John Keats, Wordsworth also goes on to make almost religious claims for poetry, asserting its obligation to speak to, uplift, and transform the general population.

Modern and contemporary writers have been perhaps less willing to define the requirements and purposes of true art than they have been to explain themselves as artists. They have analyzed their motives for writing. For example, William Saroyan proclaims in "Why I Write": "I felt impelled from the time I knew I had memory to do something about the past, about endings, about human death." These writers have described their participation in the creative process, which

> leads so wildly and originally into new territory that no judgment can at the moment be made about values, significance, and so on. I am making something new, something that has not been judged before. Later others—and maybe I myself—will make judgments. Now, I am headlong to discover. Any distraction may harm the creating.
>
> William Stafford, "Writing"

In "Writing off the Subject," the first of a series of essays on poetry writing entitled *The Triggering Town,* the poet Richard Hugo shifts from describing to prescribing the creative process:

> To write a poem you must have a streak of arrogance—not in real life I hope. In real life try to be nice. It will save you a hell of a lot of trouble and give you more time to write. By arrogance I mean that when you are writing you must assume that the next thing you put down belongs not for reasons of logic, good sense, or narrative development, but because you put it there. You, the same person who said that, also said this. The adhesive force is your way of writing, not sensible connection.

In the briefest of essays, a sort of prose poem, Marguerite Duras approaches the creative process less directly and more concretely, through the memory of a painting and then an analogy from visual art:

> No, it wasn't a Monet or a Manet. It was a Bonnard. It was at the house of some people in Berne who were great art collectors. They had a painting by Bonnard: a boat, with the wife's family in it. Bonnard always wanted to alter the sail, and because he kept on

about it they let him have the painting back. When he returned it he said he considered it finished now. But the sail had swallowed up everything, dwarfing the sea, the people in the boat and the sky. That can happen with a book: you can start a new sentence and change the whole subject. You don't notice anything; you look up at the window and it's evening. And the next morning you find you've sat down to a different book. The making of pictures and books isn't something completely conscious. And you can never, never find words for it.

EXERCISE: Writing about Writing

As a finale to your own introduction to the creative process, make a list of all your thoughts and feelings, positive and negative, about your experience with creative writing. To get you started, or keep you going, you can try answering any of the following questions:

What have you discovered about your own creativity?
Under what circumstances is it most available to you?
Can you remember and describe a moment of inspiration? of blank frustration? of surprising joy or pain?
Which pieces of your own writing are you most satisfied with? Why?
Which pieces have received the most praise from others? Do you agree?
Do you feel most comfortable in one genre? Do you have some ideas about what you would like to accomplish in that genre, what it is capable of expressing?
Do you have some of your own ideas as to what makes a "good" poem, story, or essay?
What would you like to create and communicate as a writer?
Why do you think you are motivated to write?

As the breadth of these questions suggests, you can be an authority now on creative writing. Circle those items and answers you think would most effectively establish your authority: those that suggest an original insight or trigger a flow of particularly vivid or unusual concrete details. Choose three of these insights, and begin to draft an essay to present them, drawing in as many telling details as you can.

To help yourself stay focused, you may want to establish a single question for your essay to answer: "What motivates me to write?" "What do I hope to accomplish in my writing?" "How do I write?" "What is it like to write?" Or you may wish to address two or three related questions in separate paragraphs. The passages in this chapter by experienced authors offer three possible approaches to adopt or adapt as you begin to shape your writing: the authentic personal revelation (Saroyan and Stafford); the imperative instruction qualified by humor (Hugo); and the more objective weaving of narrative and example (Duras). Feel free to display all your imaginative resources—feel free.

•   •   •

Acknowledgments (continued from copyright page)

Robert Creely: "The Flower," from *Collected Poems of Robert Creely, 1945–1975* by
   Robert Creely. Copyright © 1983 by The Regents of the University of
   California. Reprinted by permission of University of California Press.
Marguerite Duras: "Bonnard," from *Practicalities* by Marguerite Duras, translated by
   Barbara Bray. Copyright © 1990 by William Collins. Used by permission of
   Grove Press, Inc.
Lawrence Ferlinghetti: "I Am Waiting" by Lawrence Ferlinghetti, from *A Coney
   Island of the Mind.* Copyright © 1958 by Lawrence Ferlinghetti. Reprinted by
   permission of New Directions Publishing Corporation.
Robert Francis: "Silent Poem" by Robert Francis, reprinted from *Robert Francis:
   Collected Poems 1936–1976* (Amherst: University of Massachusetts Press, 1976),
   copyright © 1970 by Robert Francis.
Nan Fry: "The Plum" by Nan Fry, from *Relearning the Dark* (Washington, DC:
   Washington Writers' Publishing House, 1991). Reprinted by permission of the
   author.
Robert Haas: "Letter" by Robert Haas, from *Field Guide.* Reprinted by permission
   of Yale University Press.
John Haines: "And When the Green Man Comes" by John Haines, from *Winter
   News,* copyright 1961. Reprinted by Wesleyan University Press by permission of
   the University Press of New England.
Langston Hughes: "Dream Deferred" ("Harlem") by Langston Hughes. From *The
   Panther and the Lash.* Copyright 1951 by Langston Hughes. Reprinted by
   permission of Alfred A. Knopf, Inc.
David Ignatow: "And the Same Words" by David Ignatow. From *Poems, 1934–
   1969,* copyright 1964. Reprinted by Wesleyan University Press by permission of
   the University Press of New England.
Ted Kooser: "Abandoned Farmhouse" by Ted Kooser. Reprinted from *Sure Signs:
   New and Selected Poems.* Reprinted by permission of the University of Pittsburgh
   Press. Copyright 1980 by Ted Kooser.
Stanley Kunitz: "Indian Summer at Land's End" by Stanley Kunitz. From *The
   Poems of Stanley Kunitz, 1928–1978.* Copyright © 1971 by Stanley Kunitz. By
   permission of Little, Brown & Company.
Denise Levertov: "What Were They Like?" by Denise Levertov, from *Poems 1960–
   1967.* Copyright © 1966 by Denise Levertov Goodman. Reprinted by
   permission of New Directions Publishing Corporation.
John Logan: "Suzanne," copyright © 1989 by the John Logan Literary Estate Inc.
   Reprinted from *John Logan: The Collected Poems* by John Logan with the
   permission of BOA Editions Ltd., 92 Park Avenue, Brockport, NY, 14420.
Archibald MacLeish: From "Ars Poetica," in *New and Collected Poems 1917–1976*
   by Archibald MacLeish. Copyright © 1976 by Archibald MacLeish. Reprinted
   by permission of Houghton Mifflin Company. All rights reserved.
William Matthews: From *Rising and Falling* by William Matthews. Copyright ©
   1976 by William Matthews. First appeared in *Rapport.* By permission of Little,
   Brown & Company.
Marge Piercy: "Simple-song," copyright © 1969 by Marge Piercy. Reprinted from
   Hard Loving. Reprinted by Wesleyan University Press by permission of
   University Press of New England.

Pattiann Rogers: "The Family Is All There Is," from *Splitting and Binding* by
    Pattiann Rogers. Copyright 1989 by Pattiann Rogers. Reprinted by Wesleyan
    University Press by permission of the University Press of New England.
Anne Sexton: From "Cinderella," from *Transformations* by Anne Sexton. Copyright
    © 1971 by Anne Sexton. Reprinted by permission of Houghton Mifflin Co. All
    rights reserved.
Maura Stanton: "Childhood" by Maura Stanton. Reprinted from *Cries of Swimmers.*
    By permission of Carnegie Mellon University Press. © 1991 by Maura Stanton.
Gary Snyder: "Some Good Things to Be Said for the Iron Age" by Gary Snyder,
    from *Regarding Wave.* Copyright © 1970 by Gary Snyder. Reprinted by
    permission of New Directions Publishing Corporation.
James Tate: "Why I Will Not Get Out of Bed," © 1978 by James Tate. From *The
    Lost Pilot* by James Tate, first published by The Ecco Press in 1982. Reprinted
    by permission.
William Carlos Williams: "Nantucket," "Between Walls," and "This Is Just to Say"
    by William Carlos Williams. From *The Collected Poems of William Carlos
    Williams, 1909–1939, vol. I.* Copyright 1938 by New Directions Publishing
    Corporation. Reprinted by permission of New Directions Publishing
    Corporation.
James Wright: "Lying in a Hammock at William Duffy's Farm in Pine Island,
    Minnesota" and "In Ohio" by James Wright. From *Collected Poems,* copyright
    1961. Reprinted by Wesleyan University Press by permission of the University
    Press of New England.

Index